Theodor de Bry, John White, Thomas Harriot

A Brief and True Report of the New Found Land of Virginia

Theodor de Bry, John White, Thomas Harriot

A Brief and True Report of the New Found Land of Virginia

ISBN/EAN: 9783337320102

Printed in Europe, USA, Canada, Australia, Japan

Cover: Foto ©ninafisch / pixelio.de

More available books at **www.hansebooks.com**

Thomas Hariot, an eminent English Mathematician, was born at Oxford in the Year 1560. Having been instructed in Grammar-learning in that City, he became a Commoner of St. Mary Hall, where he took a Batchelor of Arts Degree in 1579. He had then so distinguished himself by his uncommon Skill in Mathematicks, as to be soon after recommended to Sr. Walter Raleigh as a proper Preceptor to him in that Science. Accordingly that Noble Knight became his first Patron, took him into his Family, and allowed him a handsome Pension. In 1585, he was sent over by Sr. Walter Raleigh with his first Colony to Virginia; where being settled, he was employed in discovering and Surveying that Country, and observing what Commodities it produced, together with the Manners and Customs of its Inhabitants. He published this Book, as an Account of Virginia; and it was afterwards reprinted in the third Volume of Hakluyt's Voyages. Upon his return to England, he was introduced by his Patron to the Acquaintance of Henry Earl of Northumberland, who allowed him a Pension of £120 yearly. About the same time, Mr. Robert Hues, well known by his Treatise upon the Globes, and Mr. Walter Warner, who is said to have communicated to the famous Harvey, the first hint concerning the Circulation of the Blood, being both of them Mathematicians, received Pensions from him of like value. So that in 1606, when the Earl was committed to the Tower for Life Hariot, Hues, and Warner were his constant Companions, and were usually called the Earl of Northumberland's three Magi. They had a Table at the Earl's Charge, and the Earl did constantly converse with them to divert the Melancholy of his confinement; as did also Sr. Walter Raleigh who was in the Tower at the same time. Mr. Thomas Hariot lived for some time at Sion College, and died in London July the 2d 1621, of a Cancer in his Lip. He was universally esteemed on account of his Learning. When he was but a young Man, he was stiled by Mr. Hakluyt, "Juvenis in disciplinis Mathematicis specilliens": and by Camden, "Mathematicus insignis".

TO THE RIGHT
WORTHIE AND HONOV-
RABLE, SIR VVALTER RALEGH,
KNIGHT, SENESCHAL OF THE DVCHIES OF
Cornewall and Exeter, and L. Warden of the stannaries in Deuon
and Cornewall. T.B. wisheth true felicitie.

AMORE ET VIRTVTE.

IR, seeing that the parte of the Worlde, which is betwene the
FLORIDA and the Cap BRETON nowe nammed VIRGI-
NIA, to the honneur of yours most souueraine Layde and Queene
ELIZABETZ, hath ben descouuerd by yours meanes. And
great chardges. And that your Collonye hath been theer estab-
lished to your great honnor and prayse, and noe lesser proffit vnto the common

welth: Yt ys good raifon that euery man euert we him felfe for to showe the bene-
fit which they haue receue of yt. Theerfore, for my parte I haue been'allwayes
Defirous for to make yow knowe the good will that I haue to remayne ftill your
moft humble feruant. I haue thincke that I cold faynde noe better occafion to
declare yt, then takinge the paines to cott in copper (the moft diligentye and well
that wear in my poffible to doe) the Figures which doe leuelye reprefent the forme and maner of the Jnhabitants of thefame countrye with theirs ceremonies,
follemne, feaftes, and the manner and fituation of their Townes, or Uillages.
Addinge vnto euery figure a brief declaration of thefame, to that ende that eue-
rye man cold the better vnderftand that which is in liuelye reprefented. Moreouer I haue thincke that the aforefaid figures wear of greater commendation, Jf
fomme Hiftoire which tmitinge of the commodites and fertillitye of the faid cou-
trye weare Ioyned with thefame, therfore haue I ferue mifelfe of the rapport
which Thomas Hariot hath lately fett foorth, and haue cauffe them booth togither to be printed for to dedicated vnto you, as a thinges which by reigtte doeth
allreadye apparteyne vnto you. Therfore doe I creaue that you will accept this
litle Booke, and take yt In goode partie. And defiringe that fauor that you will
receue me in the nomber of one of your moft humble feruantz, befechinge the
Lrd to blef, and further you in all yours good doinges and actions, and alfo to
preferue, and keepe you allwayes in good helthe. And foe I comitt you vnto
the almyhttie, from Franckfort the firft of Apprill 1590.

Your moft humble feruant,

THEODORVS de BRY.

TO THE ADVEN-
TVRERS, FAVORERS, AND
WELWILLERS OF THE EN-
TERPRISE FOR THE INHABITTING
and planting in VIRGINIA.

SINCE the first vndertaking by Sir Walter Ralegh to deale in the action of discouering of that Countrey which is now called and known by the name of VIRGINIA; many voyages hauing bin thither made at sundrie times to his great charge; as first in the yeere 1584. and afterwardes in the yeeres 1585. 1586. and now of late this last yeare of 1587. There haue bin diuers and variable reportes with some slaunderous and shamefull speeches bruited abroade by many that returned from thence. Especially of that discouery which was made by the Colony transported by Sir Richard Greinuile in the yeare 1585. being of all the others the most principal and as yet of most effect, the time of their abode in the countrey beeing a whole yeare, when as in the other voyage before they staied but sixe weekes; and the others after were onelie for supply and transportation, nothing more being discouered then had been before. Which reportes haue not done a litle wrong to many that otherwise would haue also fauoured & aduentured in the action, to the honour and benefite of our nation, besides the particular profite and credite which would redound to them selues the dealers therein; as I hope by the sequele of euents to the shame of those that haue auouched the contrary shalbe manifest: if you the aduenturers, fauourers, and welwillers do but either encrease in number, or in opinion continue, or hauing bin doubtfull renewe your good liking and furtherance to deale therein according to the worthinesse thereof alreadye found and as you shall vnderstand hereafter to be requisite. Touching which woorthines through cause of the diuersitie of relations and reportes, manye of your opinions coulde not bee firme, nor the mindes of some that are well disposed, bee setled in any certaintie.

I haue therefore thought it good beeing one that haue beene in the discouerie and in dealing with the naturall inhabitantes specially imploied; and hauing therefore seene and knowne more then the ordinarie: to imparte so much vnto you of the fruites of our labours, as that you may knowe howe iniuriously the enterprise is slaundered. And that in publike manner at this present chiefelie for two respectes.

First that some of you which are yet ignorant or doubtfull of the state thereof, may see that there is sufficiet cause why the cheefe enterpriser with the fauour of her Maiestie, notwithstanding such reportes; hath not onelie since continued the action by sending into the countrey againe, and replanting this last yeere a new Colony; but is also readie, according as the times and meanes will affoorde, to follow and prosecute the same.

Secondly, that you seeing and knowing the continuance of the action by the view hereof you may generally know & learne what the countrey is, & ther vpon cosider how your dealing therein if it proceede, may returne you profit and gaine; bee it either by inhabitting & planting or otherwise in furthering thereof.

And least that the substance of my relation should be doubtful vnto you as of others by reason of their diuersitie: I will first open the cause in a few wordes wherefore they are so different; referring my selfe to your fauourable constructions, and to be adiudged of as by good consideration you shall finde cause.

Of our companie that returned some for their misdemenour and ill dealing in the countrey, haue beene there worthily punished; who by reason of their badde natures, haue maliciously not onelie spoken ill of their Gouernours; but for their sakes slaundered the countrie it selfe. The like also haue those done which were of their consort.

Some beeing ignorant of the state thereof, notwithstanding since their returne amõgest their friendes and acquaintance and also others, especially if they were in compaine where they might not be gainesaide, woulde seeme to knowe so much as no men more; and make no men so great trauailers as themselues. They stood so much as it maie seeme vppon their credite and reputation that hauing been a twelue moneth in the countrey, it woulde haue beene a great disgrace vnto them as they thought, if they coulde not haue saide much wheter it were true or false. Of which some haue spoken of more then euer they saw or otherwise knew to bee there; otherfome haue not bin ashamed to make absolute denial of that which although not by thẽ, yet by others is most certainely ãd there plẽtifully knowne. And otherfome make difficulties of those things they haue no skill of.

The cause of their ignorance was, in that they were of that many that were neuer out of the Iland where wee were seated, or not farre, or at the leastwise in few places els, during the time of our aboade in the countrey; or of that many that after golde and siluer was not so soone found, as it was by them looked for, had little or no care of any other thing but to pamper their bellies; or of that many which had little vnderstanding, lesse discretion, and more tongue then was needfull or requisite.

Some also were of a nice bringing vp, only in cities or townes, or such as neuer (as I may say) had seene the world before. Because there were not to bee found any English cities, nor such faire houses, nor at their owne wish any of their olde accustomed daintie food, nor any soft beds of downe or fethers: the countrey was to them miserable, & their reports thereof according.

Because my purpose was but in briefe to open the cause of the varietie of such speeches, the particularities of them, and of many enuious, malicious, and slaũderous reports and deuises els, by our owne countrey men besides; as trifles that are not worthy of wise men to bee thought vpon, I meane not to trouble you withall: but will passe to the commodities, the substance of that which I haue to make relation of vnto you.

The treatise where of for your more readie view & easier vnderstanding I will diuide into three speciall parts. In the first I will make declaration of such commodities there alreadie found or to be raised, which will not onely serue the ordinary turnes of you which are and shall bee the planters and inhabitants, but such an ouerplus sufficiently to bee yelded, or by men of skill to bee prouided, as by way of trafficke and exchaunge with our owne nation of England, will enrich your selues the prouiders; those that shal deal with you; the enterprisers in general; and greatly profit our owne countrey men, to supply them with most things which heretofore they haue bene faine to prouide, either of strangers or of our enemies: which commodities for distinction sake, I call *Merchantable*.

In the second, I will set downe all the cõmodities which wee know the countrey by our experience doeth yeld of it selfe for victuall, and sustenance of mans life; such as is vsually fed vpon by the inhabitants of the countrey, as also by vs during the time we were there.

In the last part I will make mention generally of such other cõmodities besides, as I am able to remember, and as I shall thinke behoofull for those that shall inhabite, and plant there to knowe of; which specially concerne building, as also some other necessary vses: with a briefe description of the nature and maners of the people of the countrey.

THE FIRST PART.
OF MARCHAN-
TABLE COMMO-
DITIES.

Silke of graſſe or graſſe Silke.

Here is a kind of graſſe in the countrey vppon the blades where of there groweth very good ſilke in forme of a thin glittering skin to bee ſtript of. It groweth two foote and a halfe high or better: the blades are about two foot in length, and halfe inch broad. The like groweth in Perſia, which is in the ſelfe ſame climate as Virginia, of which very many of the ſilke workes that come from thence into Europe are made. Here of if it be planted and ordered as in Perſia, it cannot in reaſon be otherwiſe, but that there will riſe in ſhorte time great profite to the dealers therein; ſeeing there is ſo great vſe and vent thereof as well in our countrey as els where. And by the meanes of ſowing & plating in good ground, it will be farre greater, better, and more plentifull then it is. Although notwithſtanding there is great ſtore thereof in many places of the countrey growing naturally and wilde. Which alſo by proofe here in England, in making a piece of ſilke Grogran, we found to be excellent good.

Worme Silke.

In manie of our iourneyes we found ſilke wormes fayre and great; as bigge as our ordinary walnuttes. Although it hath not beene our happe to haue found ſuch plentie as elſewhere to be in the coūtrey we haue heard of, yet ſeeing that the countrey doth naturally breede and nouriſh them, there is no doubt but if art be added in plantig of mulbery trees and others fitte for them in commodious places, for their feeding and nourishing; and some of them carefully gathered and husbanded in that sort as by men of skill is knowne to be necessarie: there will rise as great profite in time to the Virginians, as there of doth now to the Persians, Turkes, Italians and Spaniards.

Flaxe and Hempe.

The trueth is that of Hempe and Flaxe there is no great store in any one place together, by reason it is not planted but as the soile doth yeeld it of it selfe; and howsoeuer the leafe, and stemme or stalke doe differ from ours: the stuffe by the iudgemēt of men of skill is altogether as good as ours. And if not, as further proofe should finde otherwise; we haue that experience of the soile, as that there cannobee shewed anie reason to the contrary, but that it will grow there excellent well, and by planting will be yeelded plentifully seeing there is so much ground whereof some may well be applyed to such purposes. What benefite heereof may growe in cordage and linnens who can not easily vnderstand?

Allum.

There is a veine of earth along the sea coast for the space of fourtie or fiftie miles, whereof by the iudgement of some that haue made triall heere in England, is made good Allum, of that kinde which is called Roche Allum. The richnesse of such a commoditie is so well knowne that I neede not to saye any thing thereof. The same earth doth also yeelde White Copresse, Nitrum, and Alumen Plumeum, but nothing so plentifully as the common Allum; which be also of price and profitable.

Wapeih.

Wapeih, a kinde of earth so called by the naturall inhabitants; very like to terra sigillata: and hauing beene refined, it hath beene found by some of our Phisitiōs and Chirurgeons to bee of the same kinde of vertue and more effectuall. The inhabitāts vse it very much for the cure of sores and woundes: there is in diuers places great plentie, and in some places of a blewe sort.

Pitch, Tarre, Rozen, and Turpentine.

There are those kindes of trees which yeelde them abundantly and great store. In the very same Iland where wee were seated, being fifteene miles of length, and fiue or sixe miles in breadth, there are fewe trees els but of the same kind; the whole Iland being full.

Sassafras.

Of the new found land of Virginia.

Sassafras.

Sassafras, called by the inhabitantes *Winauk*, a kinde of wood of most pleasand and sweete smel; and of most rare vertues in phisick for the cure of many diseases. It is found by experience to bee farre better and of more vses then the wood which is called *Guaiacum*, or *Lignum vitæ*. For the description, the manner of vsing and the manifolde vertues thereof, I referre you to the booke of *Monardus*, translated and entituled in English, *The ioysull newes from the West Indies*.

Cedar.

Cedar, a very sweet wood & fine timber; wherof if nests of chests be there made, or timber therof fitted for sweet & fine bedsteads, tables, deskes, lutes, virginalles & many things else, (of which there hath beene proofe made already) to make vp fraite with other principal commodities will yeeld profite.

Wine.

There are two kinds of grapes that the soile doth yeeld naturally: the one is small and sowre of the ordinarie bignesse as ours in England: the other farre greater & of himselfe iushious sweet. When they are plāted and husbandeg as they ought, a principall commoditie of wines by them may be raised.

Oyle.

There are two sortes of *Walnuttes* both holding oyle, but the one farre more plentifull then the other. When there are milles & other deuises for the purpose, a commodity of them may be raised because there are infinite store. There are also three seuerall kindes of *Berries* in the forme of Oke akornes, which also by the experience and vse of the inhabitantes, wee finde to yeelde very good and sweete oyle. Furthermore the *Beares* of the countrey are commonly very fatte, and in some places there are many: their fatnesse because it is so liquid, may well be termed oyle, and hath many speciall vses.

Furres:

All along the Sea coast there are great store of *Otters*, which beeyng taken by weares and other engines made for the purpose, will yeelde good profite. Wee hope also of *Marterne furres*, and make no doubt by the relation of the people but that in some places of the countrey there are store: although there were but two skinnes that came to our handes. *Luzarnes* also we haue vnderstāding of, although for the time we saw none.

b

Deare skinnes.

Deare skinnes dressed after the manner of *Chamoes* or vndressed are to be had of the naturall inhabitants thousands yeerely by way of trafficke for trifles: and no more wast or spoile of Deare then is and hath beene ordinarily in time before.

Ciuet cattes.

In our trauailes, there was founde one to haue beene killed by a saluage or inhabitant: and in an other place the smell where one or more had lately beene before, whereby we gather besides then by the relation of the people that there are some in the countrey: good profite will rise by them.

Iron.

In two places of the countrey specially, one about fourescore and the other sixe score miles from the Fort or place where wee dwelt: wee founde neere the water side the ground to be rockie, which by the triall of a minerall man, was founde to holde Iron richly. It is founde in manie places of the countrey else. I knowe nothing to the contrarie, but that it maie bee allowed for a good marchantable commoditie, considering there the small charge for the labour and feeding of men: the infinite store of wood: the want of wood and deerenesse thereof in England: & the necessity of ballasting of shippes.

Copper.

A hundred and fiftie miles into the maine in two townes wee founde with the inhabitaunts diuerse small plates of copper, that had beene made as wee vnderstood, by the inhabitantes that dwell farther into the countrey: where as they say are mountaines and Riuers that yeelde also whyte graynes of Mettall, which is to bee deemed *Siluer*. For confirmation whereof at the time of our first arriuall in the Countrey, I sawe with some others with mee, two small peeces of siluer grosly beaten about the weight of a Testrone, hangyng in the eares of a *Wiroans* or *chiefe Lorde* that dwelt about fourescore myles from vs; of whom thorowe enquiry, by the number of dayes and the way, I learned that it had come to his handes from the same place or neere, where I after vnderstood the copper was made and the white graynes of mettall founde. The aforesaide copper wee also founde by triall to holde siluer.

Pearle.

Sometimes in feeding on muscles wee founde some pearle; but it was our hap to meete with ragges, or of a pide colour, not hauing yet discouered those places

Of the new found land of Virginia.   11

places where wee hearde of better and more plentie. One of our companie; a man of skill in such matters, had gathered together from among the sauage people aboute fiue thousande: of which number he chose so many as made a fayre chaine, which for their likenesse and vniformitie in roundnesse, orientnesse, and pidenesse of many excellent colours, with equalitie in greatnesse, were verie fayre and rare; and had therefore beene presented to her Maiestie, had wee not by casualtie and trough extremity of a storme, lost them with many things els in comming away from the countrey.

Sweete Gummes.

Sweete Gummes of diuers kindes and many other Apothecary drugges of which wee will make speciall mention, when wee shall receiue it from such men of skill in that kynd, that in taking reasonable paines shall discouer them more particularly then wee haue done; and than now I can make relation of, for want of the examples I had prouited and gathered, and are nowe lost, with other thinges by causualtie before mentioned.

Dyes of diuers kindes.

There is Shoemake well knowen, and vsed in England for blacke; the seede of an hearbe called Wasewówr; little small rootes called Cháppacor; and the barke of the tree called by the inhabitaunts Tangomóckonomindge: which Dies are for diuers sortes of red: their goodnesse for our English clothes remayne yet to be proued. The inhabitants vse them onely for the dying of hayre, and colouring of their faces, aud Mantles made of Deare skinnes; and also for the dying of Rushes to make artificiall workes withall in their Mattes and Baskettes; hauing no other thing besides that they account of, apt to vse them for. If they will not proue merchantable there is no doubt but the Planters there shall finde apte vses for them, as also for other colours which wee knowe to be there.

Oade.

A thing of so great vent and vse amongst English Diers, which cannot bee yeelded sufficiently in our owne countrey for spare of ground; may bee planted in Virginia, there being ground enough. The grouth therof need not to be doubted when as in the Ilandes of the Asores it groweth plentifully, which is in the same climate. So likewise of Madder.

Suger canes.

Whe carried thither Suger canes to plant which beeing not so well preserued as was requisit, & besides the time of the yere being past for their setting when we

b 2

arriued, wee could not make that proofe of them as wee defired. Notwithſtāding ſeeing that they grow in the ſame climate, in the South part of Spaine and in Barbary, our hope in reaſon may yet continue. So likewiſe for *Orenges*, and *Lemmons*, there may be planted alſo *Quinſes*. Wherbi may grow in reaſonable time if the action be diligently proſecuted, no ſmall commodities in *Sugers*, *Suckets*, and *Marmalades*.

 Many other commodities by planting may there alſo bee raiſed, which I leaue to your diſcret and gentle conſiderations: and many alſo may bee there which yet we haue not diſcouered. Two more commodities of great value one of certaintie, and the other in hope, not to be planted, but there to be raiſed & in ſhort time to be prouided and prepared, I might haue ſpecified. So likewiſe of thoſe commodities already ſet downe I might haue ſaid more; as of the particular places where they are founde and beſt to be planted and prepared: by what meanes and in what reaſonable ſpace of time they might be raiſed to profit and in what proportion, but becauſe others then welwillers might bee therewithall acquainted, not to the good of the action, I haue wittingly omitted them: knowing that to thoſe that are well diſpoſed I haue vttered, according to my promiſe and purpoſe, for this part ſufficient.

THE

Of the new found land of Virginia.   13

THE SECOND PART,
OF SVCHE COMMO-
DITIES AS VIRGINIA IS
knowne to yeelde for victuall and sustenāce of mans life, vsually fed vpon by the naturall inhabitants: as also by vs during the time of our aboad. And first of such as are sowed and husbanded.

PAGATOWR, a kinde of graine so called by the inhabitants; the same in the West Indies is called MAYZE: English men call it Guinney wheate or Turkie wheate, according to the names of the countreys from whence the like hath beene brought. The graine is about the bignesse of our ordinary English peaze and not much different in forme and shape: but of diuers colours: some white, some red, some yellow, and some blew. All of them yeelde a very white and sweete flowre: beeing vsed according to his kinde it maketh a very good bread. Wee made of the same in the countrey some mault, whereof was brued as good ale as was to bee desired. So likewise by the help of hops therof may bee made as good Beere. It is a graine of marueilous great increase; of a thousand, fifteene hundred and some two thousand fold. There are three sortes, of which two are ripe in an eleuen and twelue weekes at the most: sometimes in ten, after the time they are set, and are then of height in stalke about sixe or seuen foote. The other sort is ripe in fourteene, and is about ten foote high, of the stalkes some beare foure heads, some three, some one, and two: euery head cōtaining fiue, sixe, or seuē hundred graines within a fewe more or lesse. Of these graines besides bread, the inhabitants make victuall

b 3

eyther by parching them; or seething them whole vntill they be broken; or boyling the floure with water into a pappe.

Okindgier, called by vs *Beanes*, because in greatnesse & partly in shape they are like to the Beanes in England, sauing that they are flatter, of more diuers colours, and some pide. The leafe also of the stemme is much different. In taste they are altogether as good as our English peaze.

Wickonzówr, called by vs *Peaze*, in respect of the beanes for distinction sake, because they are much lesse; although in forme they little differ; but in goodnesse of tast much, & are far better then our English peaze. Both the beanes and peaze are ripe in tenne weekes after they are set. They make them victuall either by boyling them all to pieces into a broth; or boiling them whole vntill they bee soft and beginne to breake as is vsed in England, eyther by themselues or mixtly together: Sometime they mingle of the wheate with them. Sometime also beeing whole sodden, they bruse or pound them in a morter, & thereof make loaues or lumps of dowishe bread, which they vse to eat for varietie.

Macócqwer, according to their seuerall formes called by vs, *Pompions*, *Mellions*, and *Gourdes*, because they are of the like formes as those kindes in England. In *Virginia* such of seueral formes are of one taste and very good, and do also spring from one seed. There are of two sorts; one is ripe in the space of a moneth, and the other in two monetas.

There is an hearbe which in Dutch is called *Melden*. Some of those that I describe it vnto, take it to be a kinde of Orage; it groweth about foure or fiue foote high: of the seede thereof they make a thicke broth, and pottage of a very good taste: of the stalke by burning into ashes they make a kinde of salt earth, wherewithall many vse sometimes to season their brothes; other salte they knowe not. Wee our selues, vsed the leaues also for pothearbes.

There is also another great hearbe in forme of a Marigolde, about sixe foote in height; the head with the floure is a spanne in breadth. Some take it to bee *Planta Solis*: of the seedes heereof they make both a kinde of bread and broth.

All the aforesaide commodities for victuall are set or sowed, sometimes in groundes a part and seuerally by themselues, but for the most part together in one ground mixtly: the manner thereof with the dressing and preparing of the groud, because I will note vnto you the fertilitie of the soile; I thinke good briefly to describe.

The ground they neuer fatten with mucke, dounge or any other thing; neither plow nor digge it as we in England, but onely prepare it in sort as followeth. A fewe daies before they sowe or set, the men with wooden instruments, made almost in forme of mattockes or hoes with long handles; the women with short peckers or parers, because they vse them sitting, of a foote long and about fiue inches in breadth: doe onely breake the vpper part of the ground to rayse vp the weedes, grasse, & old stubbes of corne stalkes with their rootes. The which after a day or twoes

drying

Of the new found land of Virginia.   15

drying in the Sunne, being scrapte vp into many small heapes, to saue them labour for carrying them away; they burne into ashes. (And whereas some may thinke that they vse the ashes for to better the grounde; I say that then they woulde eyther disperse the ashes abroade; which wee obserued they doe not, except the heapes bee too great: or els would take speciall care to set their corne where the ashes lie, which also wee finde they are carelesse of.) And this is all the husbanding of their ground that they vse.

Then their setting or sowing is after this maner. First for their corne, beginning in one corner of the plot, with a pecker they make a hole, wherein they put foure graines with that care they touch not one another, (about an inch asunder) and couer them with the moulde againe: and so through out the whole plot, making such holes and vsing them after such maner: but with this regard that they bee made in rankes, euery rake differing from other halfe a fadome or a yarde, and the holes also in euery ranke, as much. By this meanes there is a yarde spare ground betwene euery hole: where according to discretion here and there, they set as many Beanes and Peaze: in diuers places also among the seedes of *Macócqwer*, *Melden* and *Planta Solis*.

The ground being thus set according to the rate by vs experimented, an English Acre conteining fourtie pearches in length, and foure in breadth, doeth there yeeld in croppe or oscome of corne beanes, and peaze, at the least two hūdred London bushelles: besides the *Macócqwer*, *Melden*, and *Planta Solis*. When as in England fourtie bushelles of our wheate yeelded out of such an acre is thought to be much.

I thought also good to note this vnto you, if you which shall inhabite and plant there, maie know how specially that countrey corne is there to be preferred before ours: Besides the manifold waies in applying it to victuall, the increase is so much that small labour and paines is needful in respect that must be vsed for ours. For this I can assure you that according to the rate we haue made proofe of, one man may prepare and husbane so much grounde (hauing once borne corne before) with lesse thē foure and twentie houres labour, as shall yeelde him victuall in a large proportiō for a twelue mōeth, if hee haue nothing else, but that which the same groūd will yeelde, and of that kinde onelie which I haue before spoken of: the saide groūd being also but of fiue and twentie yards square. And if neede require, but that there is ground enough, there might be raised out of one and the selfsame ground two haruestes or oscomes; for they sowe or set and may at anie time when they thinke good from the middest of March vntill the ende of Iune: so that they also set when they haue eaten of their first croppe. In some places of the countrey notwithstanding they haue two haruests, as we haue heard, out of one and the same ground.

For English corne neuerthelesse whether to vse or not to vse it, you that inhabite maie do as you shall haue farther cause to thinke best. Of the grouth you need not to doubt: for barlie, oates and peaze, we haue seene proof of, not beeing purposely

b 4

sowen but fallen casually in the worst sort of ground, and yet to be as faire as any we haue euer seene here in England. But of wheat because it was musty and hat taken salt water wee could make no triall: and of rye we had none. Thus much haue I digressed and I hope not vnnecessarily: nowe will I returne againe to my course and intreate of that which yet remaineth appertaining to this Chapter.

There is an herbe which is sowed a part by it selfe & is called by the inhabitants Vppówoc: In the West Indies it hath diuers names, according to the seuerall places & countries where it groweth and is vsed: The Spaniardes generally call it Tobacco. The leaues thereof being dried and brought into powder: they vse to take the fume or smoke thereof by sucking it through pipes made of claie into their stomacke and heade; from whence it purgeth superfluous fleame & other grosse humors, openeth all the pores & passages of the body: by which meane. the vse thereof, not only preserueth the body from obstructiõs, but also if any be, so that they haue not beene of too long continuance, in short time breaketh them: wherby their bodies are notably preserued in health, & know not many greeuous diseases wherewithall wee in England are oftentimes afflicted.

This Vppówoc is of so precious estimation amongest then, that they thinke their gods are maruelously delighted therwith. Wherupon sometime they make hallowed fires & cast some of the pouder therein for a sacrifice: being in a storme vppon the waters, to pacifie their gods, they cast some vp into the aire and into the water: so a weare for fish being newly set vp, they cast some therein and into the aire: also after an escape of danger, they cast some into the aire likewise: but all done with strange gestures, stamping, somtime dauncing, clapping of hands, holding vp of hands, & staring vp into the heauens, vttering therewithal and chattering strange words & noises.

We our selues during the time we were there vsed to suck it after their maner, as also since our returne, & haue found maine rare and wonderful experiments of the vertues thereof; of which the relation woulde require a volume by it selfe: the vse of it by so manie of late, men & women of great calling as else, and some learned Phisitions also, is sufficient witnes.

And these are all the commodities for sustenance of life that I know and can remember they vse to husband: all else that followe are founde growing naturally or wilde.

Of Rootes.

OPENAVK are a kind of roots of round forme, some of the bignes of walnuts, some far greater, which are found in moist & marish grounds growing many together one by another in ropes, or as thogh they were fastnened with a string. Being boiled or sodden they are very good meate.

OKEEPENAVK are also of round shape, found in dry grounds: some are
of the

Of the new found land of Virginia.

of the bignes of a mans head. They are to be eaten as they are taken out of the ground, for by reason of their drinesse they will neither roste nor seeth. Their tast is not so good as of the former rootes, notwithstanding for want of bread & sometimes for varietie the inhabitants vse to eate them with fish or flesh, and in my iudgement they doe as well as the houshold bread made of rie heere in England.

Kaishúcpenauk, a white kind of roots about the bignes of hen egs & nere of that forme: their tast was not so good to our seeming as of the other, and therfore their place and manner of growing not so much cared for by vs: the inhabitāts notwithstanding vsed to boile & eate many.

Tsinaw a kind of roote much like vnto the which in England is called the *China root* brought from the East Indies. And we know not anie thing to the cōtrary but that it maie be of the same kind. These roots grow manie together in great clusters and doe bring foorth a brier stalke, but the leafe in shape far vnlike, which beeing supported by the trees it groweth neerest vnto, wil reach or climbe to the top of the highest. From these roots while they be new or fresh beeing chopt into small pieces & stampt, is strained with water a iuice that maketh bread, & also being boiled, a very good spoonemeate in maner of a gelly, and is much better in tast if it bee tempered with oyle. This *Tsinaw* is not of that sort which by some was caused to be brought into England for the *China roote*, for it was discouered since, and is in vse as is afore saide: but that which was brought hither is not yet knowne neither by vs nor by the inhabitants to serue for any vse or purpose, although the roores in shape are very like.

Coscúshaw, some of our company tooke to bee that kinde of roote which the Spaniards in the West Indies call *Cassauy*, whereupon also many called it by that name: it groweth in very muddie pooles and moist groundes. Being dressed according to the countrey maner, it maketh a good bread, and also a good spoonemeate, and is vsed very much by the inhabitants: The iuice of this root is poison, and therefore heede must be taken before any thing be made therewithal: Either the rootes must bee first sliced and dried in the Sunne, or by the fire, and then being pounded into floure wil make good bread: or els while they are greene they are to bee pared, cut into pieces and stampt, loues of the same to be laid neere or ouer the fire vntill it be soure, and then being well pounded againe, bread, or spone meate very good in taste, and holsome may be made thereof.

Habascon is a roote of hoat taste almost of the forme and bignesse of a Parseneepe, of it selfe it is no victuall, but onely a helpe beeing boiled together with other meates.

There are also *Leekes* differing little from ours in England that grow in many places of the countrey, of which, when we came in places where, wee gathered and eate many, but the naturall inhabitants neuer.

A briefe ant true report,
Of Fruites.

CHESTNVTS, there are in diuers places great store: some they vse to eate rawe, some they stampe and boile to make spoonemeate, and with some being sodden they make such a manner of dowe bread as they vse of their beanes before mentioned.

WALNVTS: There are two kindes of Walnuts, and of then infinit store: In many places where very great woods for many miles together the third part of trees are walnuttrees. The one kind is of the same taste and forme or litle differing from ours of England, but that they are harder and thicker shelled: the other is greater and hath a verie ragged and harde shell: but the kernell great, verie oylie and sweete. Besides their eating of them after our ordinarie maner, they breake them with stones and pound them in morters with water to make a milk which they vse to put into some sorts of their spoonmeate; also among their sodde wheat, peaze, beanes and pompions which maketh them haue a farre more pleasant taste.

MEDLARS a kind of verie good fruit, so called by vs chieflie for these respectes: first in that they are not good vntill they be rotten: then in that they open at the head as our medlars, and are about the same bignesse: otherwise in taste and colour they are farre differēt: for they are as red as cheries and very sweet: but whereas the cherie is sharpe sweet, they are lushious sweet.

METAQVESVNNAVK, a kinde of pleasaunt fruite almost of the shape & bignes of English peares, but that they are of a perfect red colour as well within as without. They grow on a plant whose leaues are verie thicke and full of prickles as sharpe as needles. Some that haue bin in the Indies, where they haue seen that kind of red die of great price which is called Cochinile to grow, doe describe his plant right like vnto this of Metaquesunnauk but whether it be the true Cochinile or a bastard or wilde kind, it cannot yet be certified. seeing that also as I heard, Cochinile is not of the fruite but founde on the leaues of the plant; which leaues for such matter we haue not so specially obserued.

GRAPES there are of two sorts which I mentioned in the marchantable cōmodities.

STRABERIES there are as good & as great as those which we haue in our English gardens.

MVLBERIES, Applecrabs, Hurts or Hurtleberies, such as wee haue in England.

SACQVENVMMENER a kinde of berries almost like vnto capres but somewhat greater which grow together in clusters vpon a plant or herb that is found in shalow waters: being boiled eight or nine hours according to their kind are very good meate and holesome, otherwise if they be eaten they will make a man for the time franticke or extremely sicke.

There is a kind of reed which beareth a seed almost like vnto our rie or wheat, & being boiled is good meate.

Of the new found land of Virginia.

In our trauailes in some places wee founde *wilde peaze* like vnto ours in England but that they were lesse, which are also good meate.

Of a kinde of fruite or berrie in forme of Acornes.

There is a kind of berrie or acorne, of which there are fiue sorts that grow on seuerall kinds of trees; the one is called *Sagatémener*, the second *Osamener*, the third *Pummuckóner*. These kind of acorns they vse to drie vpon hurdles made of reeds with fire vnderneath almost after the maner as we dry malt in England. When they are to be vsed they first water them vntil they be soft & then being sod they make a good victuall, either to eate so simply, or els being also pounded, to make loaues or lumpes of bread. These be also the three kinds of which, I said before, the inhabitants vsed to make sweet oyle.

An other sort is called *Sapúmmener* which being boiled or parched doth eate and taste like vnto chestnuts. They sometime also make bread of this sort.

The fifth sort is called *Mangúmmenauk*, and is the acorne of their kind of oake, the which beeing dried after the maner of the first sortes, and afterward watered they boile them, & their seruants or sometime the chiefe thēselues, either for variety or for want of bread, doe eate them with their fish or flesh.

Of Beastes.

Deare, in some places there are great store: neere vnto the sea coast they are of the ordinarie bignes as ours in England, & some lesse: but further vp into the countrey where there is better feed they are greater: they differ from ours onely in this, their tailes are longer and the snags of their hornes looke backward.

Conies, Those that we haue seen & al that we can heare of are of a grey colour like vnto hares: in some places there are such plétie that all the people of some townes make them mantles of the furre or flue of the skinnes of those they vsually take.

Saquenúckot & *Maquówoc*; two kindes of small beastes greater then conies which are very good meat. We neuer tooke any of them our selues, but sometime eate of such as the inhabitants had taken & brought vnto vs.

Squirels which are of a grey colour, we haue taken & eaten.

Beares which are all of black colour. The beares of this countrey are good meat; the inhabitants in time of winter do vse to take & eate manie, so also sometime did wee. They are taken cōmonlie in this sort. In some Ilands or places where they are, being hunted for, as soone as they haue spiall of a man they presently run awaie, & then being chased they clime and get vp the next tree they can, from whence with arrowes they are shot downe starke dead, or with those wounds that they may after easily bekilled, we sometime shotte them downe with our caleeuers.

I haue the names of eight & twenty seuerall sortes of beasts which I haue heard of to be here and there dispersed in the countrie, especially in the maine: of which there are only twelue kinds that we haue yet discouered, & of those that be good meat we know only them before mentioned. The inhabitants somtime kil the *Lyon* & eat him: & we somtime as they came to our hands of their Wolues or *woluish Dogges*, which I haue not set downe for good meat, least that some woulde vnderstand my iudgement therin to be more simple than needeth, although I could alleage the difference in taste of those kindes from ours, which by some of our company haue beene experimented in both.

Of Foule.

Turkie cockes and *Turkie hennes*: *Stockdoues*: *Partridges*: *Cranes*: *Hernes*: & in winter great store of *Swannes* & *Geese*. Of al sortes of foule I haue the names in the countrie language of fourescore and sixe of which number besides those that be named, we haue taken, eaten, & haue the pictures as they were there drawne with the names of the inhabitaunts of seuerall strange sortes of water foule eight, and seuenteene kinds more of land foul, although wee haue seen and eaten of many more, which for want of leasure there for the purpose coulde not bee pictured: and after wee are better furnished and stored vpon further discouery, with their strange beastes. fishe, trees, plants, and hearbes, they shall bee also published.

There are also *Parats*, *Fauleons*, & *Marlin haukes*, which although with vs they bee not vsed for meate, yet for other causes I thought good to mention.

Of Fishe.

For foure monethes of the yeere, February, March, Aprill and May, there are plentie of *Sturgeons*: And also in the same monethes of *Herrings*, some of the ordinary bignesse as ours in England, but the most part farre greater, of eighteene, twentie inches, and some two foote in length and better, both these kindes of fishe in those monethes are most plentifull, and in best seafon, which wee founde to bee most delicate and pleasaunt meate.

There are also *Troutes*, *Porpoises*, *Rayes*, *Oldwiues*, *Mullets*, *Plaice*, and very many other sortes of excellent good fish, which we haue taken & eaten, whose names I know not but in the countrey language; wee haue of twelue sorts more the pictures as they were drawn in the countrey with their names.

The inhabitants vse to take then two maner of wayes, the one is by a kind of wear made of reedes which in that countrey are very strong. The other way which is more strange, is with poles made sharpe at one ende, by shooting them into the fish after the maner as Irishmen cast dartes; either as they are rowing in their boates or els as they are wading in the shallowes for the purpose.

There

Of the new found land of Virginia.   21

There are also in many places plentie of these kindes which follow.

Sea crabbes, such as we haue in England.

Oysters, some very great, and some small; some rounde and some of a long shape: They are founde both in salt water and brackish, and those that we had out of salt water are far better than the other as in our owne countrey.

Also *Muscles, Scalopes, Periwinkles*, and *Creuses*.

Seekanauk, a kinde of crustie shell fishe which is good meate, about a foote in breadth, hauing a crustie tayle, many legges like a crab, and her eyes in her backe. They are founde in shallowes of salt waters, and sometime on the shoare.

There are many *Tortoyses* both of lande and sea kinde, their backes & bellies are shelled very thicke; their head, feete, and taile, which are in appearance, seeme ougly as though they were membres of a serpent or venemous: but notwithstanding they are very good meate, as also their egges. Some haue bene founde of a yard in bredth and better.

And thus haue I made relation of all sortes of victuall that we fed vpon for the time we were in *Virginia*, as also the inhabitants themselues, as farre foorth as I knowe and can remember or that are specially worthy to bee remembred.

THE THIRD AND
LAST PART,

OF SVCH OTHER
THINGES AS IS BE HOO-
full for those which shall plant and inhabit to
know of; with a description of the nature
and manners of the people of
the countrey.

*Of commodities for building and other
necessary vses.*

Hose other things which I am more to make rehearsall of, are such as concerne building, and other mechanicall necessarie vses; as diuers sortes of trees for house & ship timber, and other vses els: Also lime, stone, and brick, least that being not mentioned some might haue bene doubted of, or by some that are malicious reported the contrary.

  Okes, there are as faire, straight, tall, and as good timber as any can be, and also great store, and in some places very great.

 Walnut trees, as I haue saide before very many, some haue bene seen excellent faire timber of foure & fiue fadome, & aboue fourescore foot streight without bough.

 Firre trees fit for masts of ships, some very tall & great.

Rakiock,

Of the new found land of Virginia.   23

Rakiock, a kind of trees so called that are sweet wood of which the inhabitants that were neere vnto vs doe commonly make their boats or Canoes of the form of trowes; only with the helpe of fire, hatchets of stones, and shels; we haue known some so great being made in that sort of one tree that they haue carried well xx. men at once, besides much baggage: the timber being great, tal, streight, soft, light, & yet tough enough I thinke (besides other vses) to be fit also for masts of ships.

Cedar, a sweet wood good for seelings, Chests, Boxes, Bedsteedes, Lutes, Virginals, and many things els, as I haue also said before. Some of our company which haue wandered in some places where I haue not bene, haue made certaine affirmation of *Cyprus* which for such and other excellent vses, is also a wood of price and no small estimation.

Maple, and also *Wich-hazle*, wherof the inhabitants vse to make their bowes.

Holly a necessary thing for the making of birdlime.

Willowes good for the making of weares and weeles to take fish after the English manner, although the inhabitants vse only reedes, which because they are so strong as also flexible, do serue for that turne very well and sufficiently.

Beech and *Ashe*, good for caske, hoopes: and if neede require, plow worke, as also for many things els.

Elme.

Sassafras trees.

Ascopo a kinde of tree very like vnto Lawrell, the barke is hoat in tast and spicie, it is very like to that tree which Monardus describeth to bee *Cassia Lignea* of the West Indies.

There are many other strange trees whose names I knowe not but in the *Virginian* language, of which I am not nowe able, neither is it so conuenient for the present to trouble you with particular relatio: seeing that for timber and other necessary vses I haue named sufficient: And of many of the rest but that they may be applied to good vse, I know no cause to doubt.

Now for Stone, Bricke and Lime, thus it is. Neere vnto the Sea coast where wee dwelt, there are no kinde of stones to bee found (except a fewe small pebbles about foure miles off) but such as haue bene brought from farther out of the maine. In some of our voiages wee haue seene diuers hard raggie stones, great pebbles, and a kinde of grey stone like vnto marble, of which the inhabitants make their hatchets to cleeue wood. Vpon inquirie wee heard that a little further vp into the Countrey were of all sortes verie many, although of Quarries they are ignorant, neither haue they vse of any stone whereupon they should haue occasion to seeke any. For if euerie housholde haue one or two to cracke Nuttes, grinde shelles, whet copper, and sometimes other stones for hatchets, they haue enough: neither vse they any digging, but onely for graues about three foote deepe: and therefore no maruaile that they know neither Quarries, nor lime stones, which both may bee in places neerer than they wot of.

C 2

A briefe and true report,

In the meane time vntill there bee discouerie of sufficient store in some place or other conuenient, the want of you which are and shalbe the planters therein may be as well supplied by Bricke: for the making whereof in diuers places of the countrey there is clay both excellent good, and plentie; and also by lime made of Oister shels, and of others burnt, after the maner as they vse in the Iles of Tenet and Shepy, and also in diuers other places of England: Which kinde of lime is well knowne to bee as good as any other. And of Oister shels there is plentie enough: for besides diuers other particular places where are abundance, there is one shallowe sounde along the coast, where for the space of many miles together in lenght, and two or three miles in breadth, the grounde is nothing els beeing but halfe a foote or a foote vnder water for the most part.

This much can I say further more of stones, that about 120. miles from our fort neere the water in the side of a hill was founde by a Gentleman of our company, a great veine of hard ragge stones, which I thought good to remember vnto you.

Of the nature and manners of the people

It resteth I speake a word or two of the naturall inhabitants, their natures and maners, leauing large discourse thereof vntill time more conuenient hereafter: now we onely so farre foorth, as that you may know, how that they in respect of troubling our inhabiting and planting, are not to be feared; but that they shall haue cause both to feare and loue vs, that shall inhabite with them.

They are a people clothed with loose mantles made of Deere skins, & aprons of the same rounde about their middles; all els naked; of such a difference of statures only as wee in England. hauing no edge tooles or weapons of yron or steele to offend vs withall, neither know they how to make any: those weapõs that they haue are onlie bowes made of Witch hazle, & arrowes of reeds; flat edged truncheons also of wood about a yard long, neither haue they any thing to defend themselues but targets made of barcks, and some armours made of stickes wickered together with thread.

Their townes are but small, & neere the sea coast but few, some cõtaining but 10. or 12. houses: some 20. the greatest that we haue seene haue bene but of 30. houses: if they be walled it is only done with barks of trees made fast to stakes, or els with poles onely fixed vpright and close one by another.

Their houses are made of small poles made fast at the tops in rounde forme after the maner as is vsed in many arbories in our gardens of England, in most townes couered with barkes, and in some with artificiall mattes made of long rushes; from the tops of the houses downe to the ground. The length of them is commonly double to the breadth, in some places they are but 12. and 16. yardes long, and in other some wee haue seene of foure and twentie.

Of the new found land of Virginia. 25

In some places of the countrey one onely towne belongeth to the gouernment of a *Wiróans* or chiefe Lorde; in other some two or three, in some sixe, eight, & more; the greatest *Wiróans* that yet we had dealing with had but eighteene townes in his gouernmēt, and able to make not aboue seuen or eight hundred fighting men at the most: The language of euery gouernment is different from any other, and the farther they are distant the greater is the difference.

Their maner of warres amongst themselues is either by sudden surprising one an other most commonly about the dawning of the day, or moone light; or els by ambushes, or some suttle deuises: Set battels are very rare, except it fall out where there are many trees, where eyther part may haue some hope of defence, after the deliuerie of euery arrow, in leaping behind some or other.

If there fall out any warres betweē vs & them, what their fight is likely to bee, we hauing aduantages against them so many maner of waies, as by our discipline, our strange weapons and deuises els; especially by ordinance great and small, it may be easily imagined; by the experience we haue had in some places, the turning vp of their heeles against vs in running away was their best defence.

In respect of vs they are a people poore, and for want of skill and iudgement in the knowledge and vse of our things, doe esteeme our trifles before thinges of greater value: Notwithstanding in their proper manner considering the want of such meanes as we haue, they seeme very ingenious; For although they haue no such tooles, nor any such craftes, sciences and artes as wee; yet in those thinges they doe, they shewe excellencie of wit. And by howe much they vpon due consideration shall finde our manner of knowledges and craftes to exceede theirs in perfection, and speed for doing or execution, by so much the more is it probable that they shoulde desire our friendships & loue, and haue the greater respect for pleasing and obeying vs. Whereby may bee hoped if meanes of good gouernment bee vsed, that they may in short time be brought to ciuilitie, and the imbracing of true religion.

Some religion they haue alreadie, which although it be farre from the truth, yet beyng at it is, there is hope it may bee the easier and sooner reformed.

They beleeue that there are many Gods which they call *Mantóac*, but of different sortes and degrees; one onely chiefe and great God, which hath bene from all eternitie. Who as they affirme when hee purposed to make the worlde, made first other goddes of a principall order to bee as meanes and instruments to bee vsed in the creation and gouernment to follow; and after the Sunne, Moone, and Starres, as pettie goddes and the instruments of the other order more principall. First they say were made waters, out of which by the gods was made all diuersitie of creatures that are visible or inuisible.

For mankind they say a woman was made first, which by the woorking of one of the goddes, conceiued and brought foorth children: And in such sort they say they had their beginning.

c 3

But how manie yeeres or ages haue paſſed ſince, they ſay they can make no relation, hauing no letters nor other ſuch meanes as we to keepe recordes of the particularities of times paſt, but onelie tradition from father to ſonne.

They thinke that all the gods are of humane ſhape, & therfore they repreſent them by images in the formes of men, which they call *Kewaſowok* one alone is called *Kewás*. Them they place in houſes appropriate or temples which they call *Mathicómuck*; Where they voorſhip, praie, ſing, and make manie times offerings vnto them. In ſome *Machicómuck* we haue ſeene but on *Kewas*, in ſome two, and in other ſome three. The common ſort thinke them to be alſo gods.

They beleeue alſo the immortalitie of the ſoule, that after this life as ſoone as the ſoule is departed from the bodie according to the workes it hath done, it is eyther carried to heaue the habitacle of gods, there to enioy perpetuall bliſſe and happineſſe, or els to a great pitte or hole, which they thinke to bee in the furtheſt partes of their part of the worlde towarde the ſunne ſet, there to burne continually: the place they call *Popoguſſo*.

For the confirmation of this opinion, they tolde mee two ſtories of two men that had been lately dead and reuiued againe, the one happened but few yetes before our comming in the countrey of a wicked man which hauing beene dead and buried, the next day the earth of the graue beeing ſeene to moue, was takē vp againe; Who made declaration where his ſoule had beene, that is to ſaie very neere entring into *Popoguſſo*, had not one of the gods ſaued him & gaue him leaue to returne againe, and teach his friends what they ſhould doe to auoid that terrible place of torment.

The other happened in the ſame yeere wee were there, but in a towne that was threeſcore miles from vs, and it was tolde mee for ſtraunge newes that one beeing dead, buried and taken vp againe as the firſt, ſhewed that although his bodie had lien dead in the graue, yet his ſoule was aliue, ānd had trauailed farre in a long broade waie, on both ſides whereof grewe moſt delicate and pleaſaūt trees, bearing more rare and excellent fruites then euer hee had ſeene before or was able to expreſſe, and at length came to moſt braue and faire houſes, neere which hee met his father, that had beene dead before, who gaue him great charge to goe backe againe and ſhew his friendes what good they were to doe to enioy the pleaſures of that place, which when he had done he ſhould after come againe.

What ſubtilty ſoeuer be in the W*iroances* and Prieſtes, this opinion worketh ſo much in manie of the common and ſimple ſort of people that it maketh them haue great reſpect to their Gouernours, and alſo great care what they do, to auoid torment after death, and to enioy bliſſe; althought notwithſtanding there is puniſhment ordained for malefactours, as ſtealers, whoremoongers, and other ſortes of wicked doers; ſome puniſhed with death, ſome with forfeitures, ſome with beating, according to the greatnes of the factes.

And this is the ſumme of their religion, which I learned by hauing ſpecial familiarity

Of the new found land of Virginia.   27

miliarity with some of their priestes. Wherein they were not so sure grounded, nor gaue such credite to their traditions and stories but through conuersing with vs they were brought into great doubts of their owne, and no small admiratiō of ours, with earnest desire in many, to learne more than we had meanes for want of perfect vtterance in their language to expresse.

Most thinges they sawe with vs, as Mathematicall instruments, sea compasses, the vertue of the loadstone in drawing yron, a perspectiue glasse whereby was shewed manie strange sightes, burning glasses, wildefire woorkes, gunnes, bookes, writing and reading, spring clocks that seeme to goe of themselues, and manie other thinges that wee had, were so straunge vnto them, and so farre exceeded their capacities to comprehend the reason and meanes how they should be made and done, that they thought they were rather the works of gods then of men, or at the leastwise they had bin giuen and taught vs of the gods. Which made manie of them to haue such opinion of vs, as that if they knew not the trueth of god and religion already, it was rather to be had from vs, whom God so specially loued then from a people that were so simple, as they found themselues to be in comparison of vs. Whereupon greater credite was giuen vnto that we spake of concerning such matters.

Manie times and in euery towne where I came, according as I was able, I made declaration of the contentes of the Bible; that therein was set foorth the true and onelie G O D, and his mightie woorkes, that therein was contayned the true doctrine of saluation through Christ, with manie particularities of Miracles and chiefe poyntes of religion, as I was able then to vtter, and thought fitte for the time. And although I told them the booke materially & of it self was not of anie such vertue, as I thought they did conceiue, but onely the doctrine therein cōtained; yet would many be glad to touch it, to embrace it, to kisse it, to hold it to their brests and heades, and stroke ouer all their bodie with it; to shewe their hungrie desire of that knowledge which was spoken of.

The *Wiroans* with whom we dwelt called *Wingina*, and many of his people would be glad many times to be with vs at our praiers, and many times call vpon vs both in his owne towne, as also in others whither he sometimes accompanied vs, to pray and sing Psalmes; hoping thereby to bee partaker of the same effectes which wee by that meanes also expected.

Twise this *Wiroans* was so grieuously sicke that he was like to die, and as hee laie languishing, doubting of anie helpe by his owne priestes, and thinking he was in such daunger for offending vs and thereby our god, sent for some of vs to praie and bee a meanes to our God that it would please him either that he might liue or after death dwell with him in blisse, so likewise were the requestes of manie others in the like case.

On a time also when their corne began to wither by reason of a drouth which happened extraordinarily, fearing that it had come to passe by reason that in some thing they had displeased vs, many woulde come to vs & desire vs to praie to our God of England, that he would preserue their corne, promising that when it was ripe we also should be partakers of the fruite.

There could at no time happen any strange sicknesse, losses, hurtes, or any other crosse vnto them, but that they would impute to vs the cause or meanes therof for offending or not pleasing vs.

One other rare and strange accident, leauing others, will I mention before I ende, which mooued the whole countrey that either knew or hearde of vs, to haue vs in wonderfull admiration.

There was no towne where we had any subtile deuise practised against vs, we leauing it vnpunished or not reuenged (because wee sought by all meanes possible to win them by gentlenesse) but that within a few dayes after our departure from euerie such towne, the people began to die very fast, and many in short space; in some townes about twentie, in some fourtie, in some sixtie, & in one sixe score, which in trueth was very manie in respect of their numbers. This happened in no place that wee coulde learne but where wee had bene, where they vsed some practise against vs, and after such time, The disease also so strange, that they neither knew what it was, nor how to cure it, the like by report of the oldest men in the countrey neuer happened before, time out of minde. A thing specially obserued by vs as also by the naturall inhabitants themselues.

Insomuch that when some of the inhabitants which were our friends & especially the Wiroans Wingina had obserued such effects in foure or fiue towns to follow their wicked practises, they were perswaded that it was the worke of our God through our meanes, and that wee by him might kil and slai whom wee would without weapons and not come neere them.

And thereupon when it had happened that they had vnderstanding that any of their enemies had abused vs in our iourneyes, hearing that wee had wrought no reuenge with our weapons, & fearing vpon some cause the matter should so rest: did come and intreate vs that we woulde bee a meanes to our God that they as others that had dealt ill with vs might in like sort die, alleaging howe much it would be for our credite and profite, as also theirs; and hoping furthermore that we would do so much at their requests in respect of the friendship we professe them.

Whose entreaties although wee shewed that they were vngodlie, affirming that our God would not subiect him selfe to anie such praiers and requestes of me: that in deede all thinges haue beene and were to be done according to his good pleasure as he had ordained: ād that we to shew our selues his true seruāts ought rather to make petition for the contrarie, that they with them might liue together with vs, bee made partakers of his truth & serue him in righteousnes; but notwithstanding in such sort, that wee referre that as all other thinges, to bee done according to his diuine will & pleasure, ād as by his wisedome he had ordained to be best.

Yet

Of the new foundland of Virginia.   29

Yet becaufe the effect fell out fo fodainly and shortly after according to their defires, they thought neuerthelesse it came to passe by our meanes, and that we in vfing such speeches vnto them did but diffemble the matter, and therefore came vnto vs to giue vs thankes in their manner that although wee fatisfied them not in promife, yet in deedes and effect we had fulfilled their defires.

This maruelous accident in all the countrie wrought fo ftrange opinions of vs, that fome people could not tel whether to think vs gods or men, and the rather becaufe that all the fpace of their ficknesse, there was no man of ours knowne to die, or that was fpecially ficke: they noted also that we had no women amongst vs, neither that we did care for any of theirs.

Some therefore were of opinion that wee were not borne of women, and therefore not mortall, but that wee were men of an old generation many yeeres paft then rifen againe to immortalitie.

Some woulde likewife feeme to prophefie that there were more of our generation yet to come, to kill theirs and take their places, as fome thought the purpofe was by that which was already done.

Thofe that were immediatly to come after vs they imagined to be in the aire, yet inuifible & without bodies, & that they by our intreaty & for the loue of vs did make the people to die in that fort as they did by shooting inuifible bullets into them.

To confirme this opinion their phifitions to excufe their ignorance in curing the difeafe, would not be ashemed to fay, but earneftly make the fimple people beleue, that the ftrings of blood that they fucked out of the ficke bodies, were the ftrings wherewithal the inuifible bullets were tied and caft.

Some alfo thought that we shot them our felues out of our pieces from the place where we dwelt, and killed the people in any fuch towne that had offended vs as we lifted, how farre diftant from vs foeuer it were.

And other fome faide that it was the fpeciall woorke of God for our fakes, as wee our felues haue caufe in fome forte to thinke no leffe, whatfoeuer fome doe or maie imagine to the contrarie, fpecially fome Aftrologers knowing of the Eclipfe of the Sunne which wee faw the fame yeere before in our voyage thytherward, which vnto them appeared very terrible. And alfo of a Comet which beganne to appeare but a few daies before the beginning of the faid ficknesse. But to exclude them from being the fpeciall an accident, there are farther reafons then I thinke fit at this prefent to bee alleadged.

Thefe their opinions I haue fet downe the more at large that it may appeare vnto you that there is good hope they may be brought through difcreet dealing and gouernement to the imbracing of the trueth, and confequently to honour, obey, feare and loue vs.

d

A briefe and true report,

And although some of our companie towardes the ende of the yeare, shewed themselues too fierce, in slaying some of the people, in some towns, vpō causes that on our part, might easily enough haue been borne withall: yet notwithstanding because it was on their part iustly deserued, the alteration of their opinions generally & for the most part concerning vs is the lesse to bee doubted. And whatsoeuer els they may be, by carefulnesse of our selues neede nothing at all to be feared.

The best neuerthelesse in this as in all actions besides is to be endeuoured and hoped, & of the worst that may happen notice to bee taken with consideration, and as much as may be eschewed.

The

Of the new found land of Virginia.

The Conclusion.

Now I haue as I hope made relation not of so fewe and smal things but that the countrey of men that are indifferent & wel disposed maie be sufficiently liked: If there were no more knowen then I haue mentioned, which doubtlesse and in great reason is nothing to that which remaineth to bee discouered, neither the soile, nor commodities. As we haue reason so to gather by the difference we found in our trauails: for although all which I haue before spoken of, haue bin discouered & experimented not far from the sea coast where was our abode & most of our trauailing: yet somtimes as we made our iourneies farther into the maine and countrey; we found the soyle to bee fatter; the trees greater and to growe thinner; the grounde more firme and deeper mould; more and larger champions, finer grasse and as good as euer we saw any in England; in some places rockie and farre more high and hillie ground; more plentie of their fruites; more abondance of beastes; the more inhabited with people, and of greater pollicie & larger dominions, with greater townes and houses.

Why may wee not then looke for in good hope from the inner parts of more and greater plentie, as well of other things, as of those which wee haue alreadie discouered? Vnto the Spaniardes happened the like in discouering the maine of the West Indies. The maine also of this countrey of *Virginia*, extending some wayes so many hundreds of leagues, as otherwise then by the relation of the inhabitants wee haue most certaine knowledge of, where yet no Christian Prince hath any possession or dealing, cannot but yeeld many kinds of excellent commodities, which we in our discouerie haue not yet seene.

What hope there is els to be gathered of the nature of the climate, being answerable to the iland of *Iapan*, the land of *China*, *Persia*, *Iury*, the Ilandes of *Cyprus* and *Candy*, the South parts of *Greece*, *Italy*, and *Spaine*, and of many other notable and famous countreis, because I meane not to be tedious, I leaue to your owne consideration.

Whereby also the excellent temperature of the ayre there at all seasons, much warmer then in England, and neuer so violently hot, as sometimes is vnder & between the Tropikes, or nere them; cannot bee vnknowne vnto you without farther relation.

For the holsomnesse thereof I neede to say but thus much: that for all the want of prouision, as first of English victuall, excepting for twentie daies, wee liued only by drinking water and by the victuall of the countrey, of which some sorts were very straunge vnto vs, and might haue bene thought to haue altered our temperatures in such sort as to haue brought vs into some greeuous and digerous diseases: secondly the want of English meanes, for the taking of beastes, fishe, and foule, which by the helpe only of the inhabitants and their meanes, coulde not bee so suddenly and easily prouided for vs, nor in so great numbers & quantities, nor of that choise as otherwise might haue bene to our better satisfaction and contentment. Some want also wee had of clothes. Furthermore, in all our trauailes which were most speciall and often in the time of winter, our lodging was in the open aire vpon the grounde. And yet I say for all this, there were but foure of our whole company (being one hundred and eight) that died all the yeere and that but at the latter ende thereof and vpon none of the aforesaide causes. For all foure especially three were feeble, weake, and sickly persons before euer they came thither, and those that knewe them much marueyled that they liued so long beeing in that case, or had aduentured to trauaile.

Seing therefore the ayre there is so temperate and holsome, the soyle so fertile and yeelding such commodities as I haue before mentioned, the voyage also thither to and fro beeing sufficiently experimented, to bee perfourmed thrise a yeere with ease and at any season thereof: And the dealing of Sir *Water Raleigh* so liberall in large giuing and graūting lande there, as is alreadie knowen, with many helpes and furtherances els: (The least that hee hath graunted hath beene fiue hundred acres to a man onely for the aduenture of his person:) I hope there remaine no cause wherby the action should be misliked.

If that those which shall thiter trauaile to inhabite and plant bee but reasonably prouided for the first yere as those are which were transported the last, and beeing there doe vse but that diligence and care as is requisite, and as they may with ease: There is no doubt but for the time following they may haue victuals that is excellent good and plentie enough; some more Englishe sortes of cattaile also hereafter, as some haue bene before, and are there yet remaining, may and shall bee God willing thiter transported: So likewise our kinde of fruites, rootes, and hearbes may bee there planted and sowed, as some haue bene alreadie, and proue wel: And in short time also they may raise of those sortes of commodities which I haue spoken of as shall both enrich them selues, as also others that shall deale with them.

And this is all the fruites of our labours, that I haue thought necessary to aduertise you of at this present: what els concerneth the nature and manners of the inhabitants of *Virginia*: The number with the particularities of the voyages thither made; and of the actions of such that haue bene by *Sir Water Raleigh* therein and there imployed, many worthy to bee remembred; as of the first discouerers of the Countrey: of our generall for the time *Sir Richard Greinuile*; and after his departure, of our Gouernour there Master *Rafe Lane*; with diuers other directed and imployed vnder theyr gouernement: Of the Captaynes and Masters of the voyages made since for transportation; of the Gouernour and assistants of those alredie transported, as of many persons, accidēts, and thinges els, I haue ready in a discourse by

Of the new foundland of Virginia.

se by it self in maner of a Chronicle according to the courfe of times, and when time shall bee thought conuenient shall be also published.

Thus referring my relation to your fauourable conftructions, expecting good fucceffe of the action, from him which is to be acknowledged the authour and gouernour not only of this but of all things els, I take my leaue of you, this moneth of Februarii, 1588.

FINIS.

THE TRVE PICTVRES AND FASHIONS OF THE PEOPLE IN THAT PARTE OF AMERICA NOVV CALLED VIRGINIA, DISCOWRED BY ENGLISMEN

sent thither in the years of our Lorde 1585. att the speciall charge and direction of the Honourable SIR WALTER RALEGH Knigt Lord Warden of the stannaries in the duchies of Corenwal and Oxford who therin hath bynne fauored and auctorised by her MAAIESTIE and her letters patents.

Translated out of Latin into English by RICHARD HACKLVIT.

DILIGENTLYE COLLECTED AND DRAOWne by IHON WHITE who was sent thiter speciallye and for the same purpose by the said SIR WALTER RALEGH the year abouesaid 1585. and also the year 1588. now cutt in copper and first published by THEODORE de BRY att his wone chardges.

THE TABLE
OF ALL DE PICTV-
RES CONTAINED IN
this Booke of Virginia.

I. The carte of all the coast of Virginia.
II. The arriuall of the Englishemen in Virginia.
III. A Weroan or great Lorde of Virginia.
IIII. On of the chieff Ladyes of Secota.
V. On of the Religeous men in the towne of Secota.
VI. A younge gentill woeman doughter of Secota.
VII. A chieff Lorde of Roanoac.
VIII. A chieff Ladye of Pomeiooc.
IX. An ageed manne in his winter garment.
X. Their manner of careynge ther Childern and a tyere of the chieffe Ladyes of the towne of Dasamonquepeuc.
XI. The Coniuerer.

XII. Their manner of makinge their Boates.
XIII. Their manner of fishynge in Virginia.
XIIII. The browyllinge of their fishe ouer the flame.
XV. Their feetheynge of their meate in earthen pottes.
XVI. Their Sitting at meate.
XVII. Their manner of prayinge with their Rattels abowt the fyer.
XVIII. Their danses whych they vse at their hyghe feastes.
XIX. The towne of Pomeiooc.
XX The towne of Secota.
XXI. Ther Idol Kiwasa.
XXII. The Tombe of their Werowans or chieff Lordes.
XXIII. The marckes of sundrye of the chiefe mene of Virginia.

To the gentle Reader.

Although (frendlye Reader) man by his disobedience, we are depriued of those good Gifts wher with he was indued in his creation, yet he was not berefte of wit to prouyde for hym selfe, nor discretion to deuise things necessarie for his vse, except suche as appartayne to his soules healthe, as may be gathered by this sauage nations, of whome this present worke intreateth. For although they haue noe true knoledge of God nor of his holye worde and are destituted of all lerninge, Yet they passe vs in many thinges, as in Sober feedinge and Dexteritye of witte, in makinge without any instrument of mettall thinges so neate and so fine, as a man would scarselye beleue thesame, Vnless the Englishemen Had made proofe Therof by their trauailes into the contrye. Consideringe, Therfore that yt was a thinge worthie of admiration, I was verye willinge to offer vnto you the true Pictures of those people wich by the helfe of Maister Richard Hakluyt of Oxford Minister of Gods Word, who first Incouraged me to publish the Worke, I creaued out of the verye original of Maister Ihon White an Englisch paynter who was sent into the contrye by the queenes Maiestye, onlye to draw the description of the place, lynelye to describe the shapes of the Inhabitants their apparell, manners of Liuinge, and fashions, att the speciall Charges of the worthy knighte, Sir WALTER RALEGH, who bestowed noe Small Sume of monnye in the serche and Discouerye of that countrye, From te yeers, 1584. to the ende of The years 1588. Morouer this booke which intreateth of that parte of the new World which the Englishemen call by the name of Virginia I heer sett out in the first place, beinge therunto requested of my Frends, by Raeson of the memorye of the fresh and laue performance ther of, albeyt I haue in hand the Historye of Florida wich should bee first sett foorthe because yt was discouured by the Frencheman longe befor the discouerye of Virginia, yet I hope shortlye also to publish thesame, A Victorye, doubtless so Rare, as I thinke the like hath not ben heard nor seene. I craeued both of them at London, an brought, Them hitherto Franckfurt, wher I and my sonnes hauen taken ernest paynes in grauinge the pictures ther of in Copper, seeing yt is a matter of noe small importance. Touchinge the stile of both the Discourses, I haue caused yt to bee Reduced into verye Good Frenche and Latin by the aide of verye worshipfull frend of myne. Finallye I hartlye Request thee, that yf any seeke to Contrefaict thes my bookx, (for in this dayes many are so malicious that they seeke to gayne by other men labours) thow wouldest giue noe credit vnto suche conterfaited Drawghte. For dyuers secret marks lye hiddin in my pictures, which wil breede Confusion vnless they bee well obserued.

The arriual of the Englishemen in Virginia.

II.

THe sea coasts of Virginia arre full of Ilåds, wehr by the entrance into the mayne låd is hard to finde. For although they bee separated with diuers and sundrie large Diuision, which seeme to yeeld conuenient entrance, yet to our great perill we proued that they wear shallowe, and full of dangerous flatts, and could neuer perce opp into the mayne låd, vntill wee made trialls in many places with or small pinness. At lengthe wee fownd an entrance vppon our mens diligent serche therof. Affter that wee had passed opp, and sayled ther in for as hort space we discouered a migthye riuer fallnige downe in to the sownde ouer against those Ilands, which neuerthelesse wee could not saile opp any thinge far by Reason of the shallewnes, the mouth ther of beinge annoyed with sands driuen in with the tyde therfore saylinge further, wee came vnto a Good bigg yland, the Inhabitante therof as soone as they saw vs began to make a great an horrible crye, as people which meuer befoer had seene men apparelled like vs, and camme a way makinge out crys like wild beasts or men out of their wyts. But beenge gentlye called backe, wee offred thē of our wares, as glasses, kniues, babies, and other trifles, which wee thougt they deligted in. Soe they stood still, and perceuinge our Good will and courtesie came fawninge vppon vs, and bade us welcome. Then they brougt vs to their village in the iland called, Roanoac, and vnto their Weroans or Prince, which entertained vs with Reasonable curtesie, althoug the wear amased at the first sight of vs. Suche was our arriuall into the parte of the world, which we call Virginia, the stature of bodee of wich people, theyr attire, and maneer of lyuinge, their feasts, and banketts, I will particullerlye declare vnto yow.

A weroan or great Lorde of Virginia. III.

THe Princes of Virginia are attyred in suche manner as is expressed in this figure. They weare the haire of their heades long and bynde opp the ende of thesame in a knot vnder thier eares. Yet they cutt the topp of their heades from the forehead to the nape of the necke in manner of a cokscombe, stirkinge a faier lõge pecher of some berd att the Begininge of the creste vppun their foreheads, and another short one on bothe seides about their eares. They hange at their eares ether thicke pearles, or somwhat els, as the clawe of some great birde, as cometh in to their fansye. Moreouer They ether pownes, or paynt their forehead, cheeks, chynne, bodye, armes, and leggs, yet in another sorte then the inhabitantz of Florida. They weare a chaine about their necks of pearles or beades of copper, wich they muche esteeme, and ther of wear they also braselets ohn their armes. Vnder their brests about their bellyes appeir certayne spotts, wheart they vse to lett them selues bloode, when they are sicke. They hange before them the skinne of some beaste verye feinelye dresset in suche sorte, that the tayle hangeth downe behynde. They carye a quiuer made of small rushes holding their bowe readie bent in on hand, and an arrowe in the other, radie to defend themselues. In this manner they goe to warr, or tho their solemne feasts and banquetts. They take muche pleasure in huntinge of deer wher of theris great store in the contrye, for yt is fruitfull, pleasant, and full of Goodly woods. Yt hathe also store of riuers full of diuers sorts of fishe. When they go to battel they paynt their bodyes in the most terible manner that thei can deuise.

On of the chieff Ladyes of Secota. IIII.

THe woemé of Secotam are of Reasonable good proportion. In their goinge they carrye their häds danglinge downe, and air dadil in a deer skinne verye excellétlye wel dressed, hanginge downe frõ their nauell vnto the mydds of their thighes, which also couereth their hynder partz. The reste of their bodies are all bare. The forr parte of their haire is cutt shorte, the rest is not ouer Longe, thinne, and softe, and falling downe about their shoulders: They weare a Wrrath about their heads. Their foreheads, cheeks, chynne, armes and leggs are pownced. About their necks they wear a chaine, ether pricked or paynted. They haue small eyes, plaine and flatt noses, narrow foreheads, and broade mowths. For the most parte they hange at their eares chaynes of longe Pearles, and of some smootht bones. Yet their nayles are not longe, as the woemen of Florida. They are also deligtted with walkinge in to the fields, 'and besides the riuers, to see the huntinge of deers and catchinge of fische.

A 2

On of the Religeous men in the towne of Secota. V.

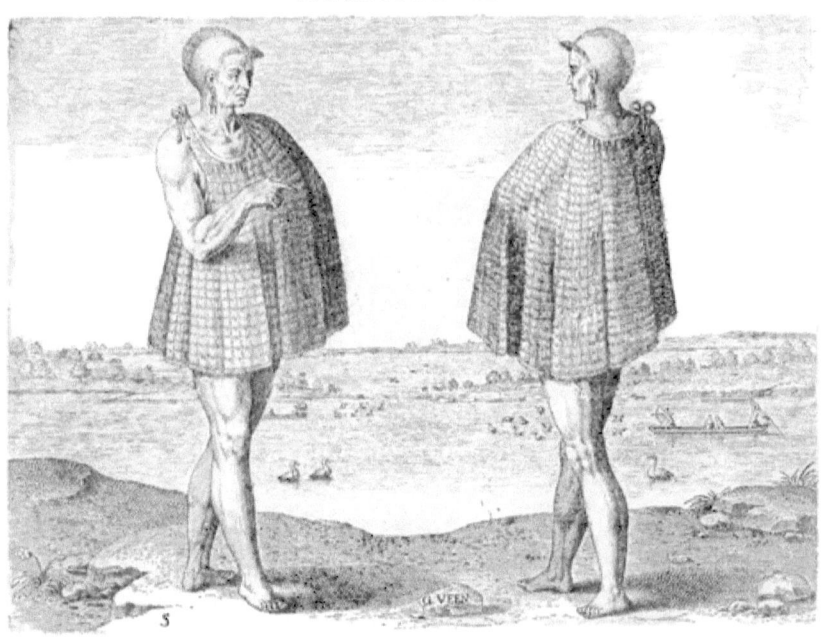

THe Priests of the aforesaid Towne of Secota are well stricken in yeers, and as yt seemeth of more experience then the comon sorte. They weare their heare cutt like a creste, on the topps of thier heades as other doe, but the rest are cutt shortte, sauinge those which growe aboue their foreheads in manner of a perriwigge. They also haue somwhat hanginge in their ears. They weare a shorte clocke made of fine hares skinnes quilted with the hayre outwarde. The rest of thier bodie is naked. They are notable enchaunters, and for their pleasure they frequent the riuers, to kill with their bowes, and catche wilde ducks, swannes, and other fowles.

A younge gentill woeman doughter VI. of Secota.

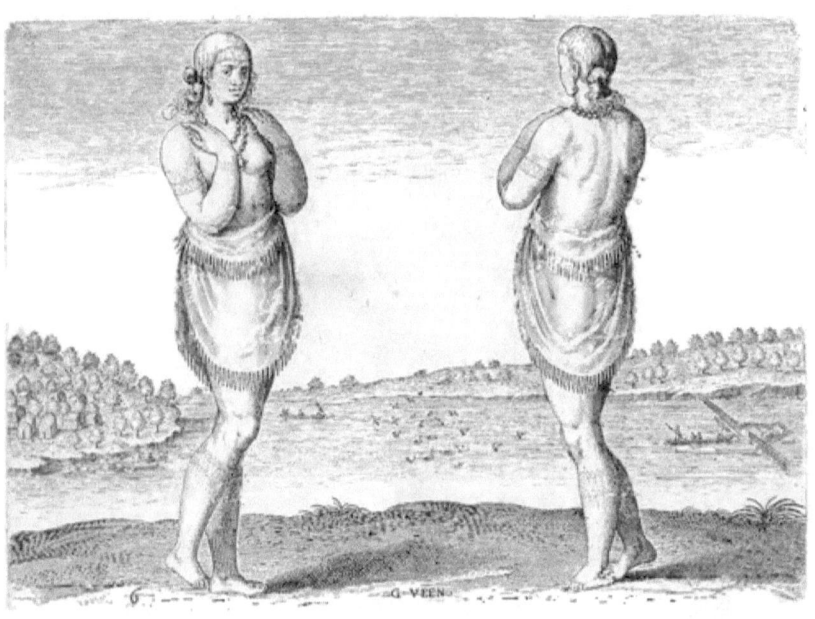

Virgins of good parentage are apparelled altogether like the woemen of Secota aboue mentionned, sauing that they weare hanginge abowt their necks in steede of a chaine certaine thicke, and rownde pearles, with little beades of copper, or polished bones betweene them. They pounce their foreheads, cheeckes, armes and legs. Their haire is cutt with two ridges aboue their foreheads, the rest is trussed opp on a knott behinde, they haue broade mowthes, reasonable fair black eyes: they lay their hands often vppon their Shoulders, and couer their brests in token of maydenlike modestye. The rest of their bodyes are naked, as in the picture is to bee seene. They deligt also in seeinge fishe taken in the riuers.

A 4

A cheiff Lorde of Roanoac. VII.

He cheefe men of the yland and towne of Roanoac reace the haire of their crounes of theyr heades cutt like a cokes còbe, as thes other doe. The rest they wear lōge as woemen and truss them opp in a knott in the nape of their necks. They hange pearles stringe copper a threed att their eares, and weare bracelets on their armes of pearles, or small beades of copper or of smoothe bone called minsal, nether paintinge nor powncings of them selues, but in token of authoritye, and honor, they wear a chaine of great pearles, or copper beades or smoothe bones abowt their necks, and a plate of copper hinge vpon a stringe, from the nauel vnto the midds of their thighes. They couer themselues before and behynde as the woemē doe with a deers skynne handsomley dressed, and fringed, More ouer they fold their armes together as they walke, or as they talke one wjth another in signe of wisdome.

The yle of Roanoac is verye pleisant, ond hath plaintie of fishe by reason of the Water that enuironeth thesame.

A cheiff Ladye of Pomeiooc. VIII.

bout 20. milles from that Iland, neere the lake of Paquippe, ther is another towne called Pomeioock hard by the sea. The apparell of the cheefe ladyes of dat towne differeth but litle from the attyre of those which lyue in Roanaac. For they weare their haire truffed opp in a knott, as the maiden doe which we fpake of before, and haue their fkinnes powneed in thefame manner, yet they wear a chaine of great pearles, or beades of copper, or fmoothe bones 5. or 6. fold obout their necks, bearinge one arme in the fame, in the other hand they carye a gourde full of fome kinde of pleafant liquor. They tye deers fkinne doubled about them crochinge hygher about their breafts, which hange downe before almoft to their knees, and are almoft altogither naked behinde. Commonlye their yonge daugters of 7. or 8. yeares olde do waigt vpon them wearinge abowt them a girdle of fkinne, which hangeth downe behinde, and is drawen vnder neath betwene their twifte, and bownde aboue their nauel with mofe of trees betwene that and thier fkinnes to couer their priuiliers withall. After they be once paft 10. yeares of age, they wear deer fkinnes as the older forte do.
They are greatlye Diligted with puppetts, and babes which wear brought oute of England.

An ageed manne in his winter garment. IX.

He aged men of Pommeioocke are couered with a large skinne which is tyed vppon their shoulders on one side and hangeth downe beneath their knees wearinge their other arme naked out of the skinne, that they maye bee at more libertie. Those skynnes are Dressed with the hair on, and lyned with other furred skinnes. The yonnge men suffer noe hairr at all to growe vppon their faces but assoone as they growe they put them away, but when thy are come to yeeres they suffer them to growe although to say truthe they come opp verye thinne. They also weare their haire bownde op behynde, and, haue a creste on their heads like the others. The contrye abowt this place is soe fruit full and good, that England is not to bee compared to yt.

B

Their manner of careynge ther Children and a tyere of the cheiffe Ladyes of the towne of Dasamonquepeuc. X.

IN the towne of Dasemonquepeuc distant from Roanoac 4. or 5. milles, the woemen are attired, and pownced, in suche sorte as the woemen of Roanoac are, yet they weare noe worathes vppon their heads, nether haue they their thighes painted with small pricks. They haue a strange manner of bearing their children, end quite contrarie to ours. For our woemen carrie their children in their armes before their brests, but they taking their sonne by the right hand, bear him on their backs, holdinge the left thighe in their lefte arme after a strange, and conuesnall fashion, as in the picture is to bee seene.

B 2

The Coniuerer.   XI.

Hey haue comonlye coniurers or iuglers which vse strange gestures, and often cõtrarie to nature in their enchantments: For they be verye familiar with deuils, of whome they enquier what their enemys doe, or other suche thinges. They shaue all their heads sauinge their creste which they weare as other doe, and fasten a small black birde aboue one of their ears as a badge of their office. They weare nothinge but a skinne which hangeth downe from their gyrdle, and couereth their priuityes. They weare a bagg by their side as is expressed in the figure.   The Inhabitants giue great credit vnto their speeche, which oftentymes they finde
to be true.

B 3

The manner of makinge their boates. XII.

He manner of makinge their boates in Virginia is verye wonderfull. For wheras they want Instruments of yron, or other like vnto ours, yet they knowe howe to make them as handsomelye, to saile with whear they liste in their Riuers, and to fishe with all, as ours. First they choose some longe, and thicke tree, according to the bignes of the boate which they would frame, and make a fyre on the grownd abowt the Roote therof, kindlinge the same by little, and little with drie mosse of trees, and chipps of woode that the flame should not mounte opp to highe, and burne to muche of the lengte of the tree. When yt is almost burnt thorough, and readye to fall they make a new fyre, which they suffer to burne vntill the tree fall of yt owne accord. Then burninge of the topp, and bowghs of the tree in suche wyse that the bodie of the same may Retayne his iust lengthe, they raise yt vppon potes laid ouer crosse wise vppon forked posts, at suche a reasonable heighte as they may handsomlye worke vppó yt. Then take they of the barke with certayne shells: thy reserue the innermost parte of the lennke, for the nethermost parte of the boate. On the other side they make a fyre according to the lengthe of the bodye of the tree, sauinge at both the endes. That which they thinke is sufficientlye burned they quenche and scrape away with shells, and makinge a new fyre they burne yt agayne, and soe they continue somtymes burninge and sometymes scrapinge, vntill the boate haue sufficient bothowmes. This god indueth thise sauage people with sufficient reason to make thinges necessarie to serue their turnes.

XIII.

Their manner of fishynge in Virginia.

They haue likewise a notable way to catche fishe in their Riuers. for whear as they lacke both yron, and steele, they faste vnto their Reedes or longe Rodds, the hollowe tayle of a certaine fishe like to a sea crabb in steede of a poynte, wehr with by nighte or day they stricke fishes, and take them opp into their boates. They also know how to vse the prickles, and pricks of other fishes. They also make weares, with settinge opp reedes or twigges in the water, which they soe plant one within a nother, that they growe still narrower, and narrower, as appeareth by this figure. Ther was neuer seene amonge vs soe cunninge a way to take fish withall, wherof sondrie sortes as they sownde in their Riuers vnlike vnto ours. which are also of a verye good taste. Dowbtless yt is a pleasant sighte to see the people, somtymes wadinge, and goinge somtymes sailinge in those Riuers, which are shallowe and not deepe, free from all care of heapinge opp Riches for their posterite, content with their state, and liuinge frendlye together of those thinges which god of his bountye hath giuen vnto them, yet without giuinge hym any thankes according to his desarte.

So sauage is this people, and depriued of the true knowledge of god. For they haue none other then is mentionned before in this worke.

The brovvyllinge of their fiſhe XIIII.
ouer the flame.

Fter they haue taken ſtore of fiſhe, they gett them vnto a place fitt to dreſs yt. Ther they ſticke vpp in the grownde 4. ſtakes in a ſquare roome, and lay 4 potes vppon them, and others ouer thwart theſame like vnto an hurdle, of ſufficient heigthe. and layinge their fiſhe vppon this hurdle, they make a fyre vnderneathe to broile the ſame, not after the manner of the people of Florida, which doe but ſchorte, and harden their meate in the ſmoke onlye to Reſerue theſame duringe all the winter. For this people reſeruinge nothinge for ſtore, thei do broile, and ſpend away all att once and when they haue further neede, they roiſte or ſeethe freſh, as wee ſhall ſee herafſter. And when as the hurdle can not holde all the fiſhes, they hange the Reſt by the fyrres on ſticks ſett vpp in the grounde againſt the fyre, and than they finiſhe the reſt of their cookerye. They take good heede that they bee not burntt. When the firſt are broyled they lay others on, that weare newlye broughte, continuinge the dreſſinge of their meate in this ſorte, vntill they thincke they haue ſufficient.

Their seetheynge of their meate in earthen pottes. XV.

Heir woemen know how to make earthen vessells with special Cunninge and that so large and fine, that our potters with lhoye wheles can make noe better: ant then Remoue them from place to place as easelye as we candoe our brassen kettles. After they haue set them vppon an heape of erthe to stay them from fallinge, they putt wood vnder which being kyndled one of them taketh great care that the fyre burne equallye Rounde abowt. They or their woemen fill the vessel with water, and then putt they in fruite, flesh, and fish, and lett all boyle together like a galliemaufrye, which the Spaniarde call, olla podrida. Then they putte yt out into dishes, and sett before the companye, and then they make good cheere together. Yet are they moderate in their eatinge wherby they auoide sicknes. I would to god wee would followe their exemple. For wee should bee free from many kynes of diseasyes which wee fall into by sumptwous and vnseasonable banketts, continuallye deuisinge new sawces, and prouocation of gluttonnye to satisfie our vnsatiable appetite.

Their sitting at meate.   XVI.

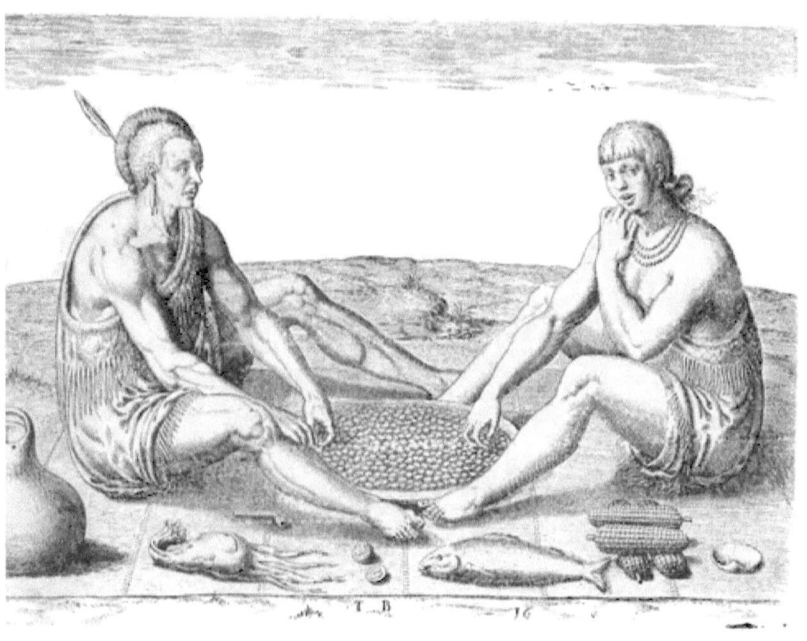

Heir manner of feeding is in this wise. They lay a matt made of bents one the grownde and sett their meate on the mids therof, and then sit downe Rownde, the men vppon one side, and the woemen on the other. Their meate is Mayz sodden, in suche forte as I described yt in the former treatise of verye good taste, deers flesche, or of some other beaste, and fishe. They are verye sober in their eatinge, and trinkinge, and consequentlye verye longe liued becausse they doe not oppress nature.

XVII.

Their manner of prainge vvith Rattels abowt te fyer.

VVhen they haue escaped any great danger by sea or lande, or be returned from the warr in token of Ioye they make a great fyer abowt which the men, and woemen sist together, holdinge a certaine fruite in their hands like vnto a rownde pompiō or a gourde, which after they haue taken out the fruits, and the seedes, then fill with smal stons or certayne bigg kernellt to make the more noise, and fasten that vppon a sticke, and singinge after their manner, they make merrie: as my selfe observed and noted downe at my beinge amonge them. For it is a strange custome, and worth the obseruation.

XVIII.

Theirdanſes vvhich they vſe att their hyghe feaſtes.

T a Certayne tyme of the yere they make a great, and ſolemne feaſte wherunto their neighbours of the townes adioninge repayre from all parts, euery man attyred in the moſt ſtrange faſhion they can deuiſe hauinge certayne marks on the backs to declare of what place they bee. The place where they meet is a broade playne, abowt the which are planted in the grownde certayne poſts carued with heads like to the faces of Nonnes couered with theyr vayles. Then beeing ſett in order they dance, ſinge, and vſe the ſtrangeſt geſtures that they can poſſiblye deuiſe. Three of the fayreſt Virgins, of the companie are in the mydds, which imbraſſinge one another doe as yt wear turne abowt in their dancinge. All this is donne after the ſunne is ſett for auoydinge of heate. When they are weerye of dancinge. they goe oute of the circle, and come in vntill their dances be ended, and they goe'to make merrye as is expreſſed in the 16. figure.

XIX.

The Tovvne of Pomeiooc.

THe townes of this contrie are in a maner like vnto thofe which are in Florida , yet are they not foe ftronge nor yet preferued with foe great care. They are compaffed abowt with poles ftarcke fafte in the grownd, but they are not verye ftronge. The entrance is verye narrowe as may be feene by this picture, which is made accordinge to the forme of the towne of Pomeiooc. Ther are but few howfes therin, faue thofe which belonge to the kinge and his nobles. On the one fide is their tempel feparated from the other howfes , and marked with the letter A. yt is builded rownde, and couered with skynne matts , and as yt wear compaffed abowt. With cortynes without windowes , and hath noe ligthe but by the doore. On the other fide is the kings lodginge marked with the letter B. Their dwellinges are builded with certaine potes faftened together , and couered with matts which they turne op as high as they thinke good, and foe receue in the lighte and other. Some are alfo couered with boughes of trees , as euery man lufteth or liketh beft. They keepe their feafts and make good cheer together in the midds of the towne as yt is defcribed in they 17. Figure. When the towne ftandeth farre from the water they digg a great poude noted with the letter C.
wherhence they fetche as muche water as
they neede.

XX.

The Tovvne of Secota.

Heir townes that are not inclosed with poles aire commonlye fayrer. Then suche as are inclosed, as apperethin this figure which liuelye expresseth the towne of Secotam. For the howses are Scattered heer and ther, and they haue gardein expressed by the letter E. wherin groweth Tobacco which the inhabitants call Vppowoc. They haue also groaues wherin thei take deer, and fields wherin they sowe their corne. In their corne fields they builde as yt weare a scaffolde wher on they sett a cottage like to a rownde chaire, signiffied by F. wherin they place one to watche. for there are suche nomber of fowles, and beasts, that vnless they keepe the better watche, they would soone deuoure all their corne. For which cause the watcheman maketh continual cryes and noyse. They sowe their corne with a certaine distance noted by H. otherwise one stalke would choke the growthe of another and the corne would not come vnto his rypeurs G. For the leaues therof are large, like vnto the leaues of great reedes. They haue also a seuerall broade plotte C. whear they meete with their neighbours, to celebrate their cheefe solemne feastes as the 18. picture doth declare: and a place D. whear after they haue ended their feaste they make merrie togither. Ouer against this place they haue a rownd plott B. wher they assemble themselues to make their solemne prayers. Not far from which place ther is a lardge buildinge A. wherin are the tombes of their kings and princes, as will appere by the 22. figure likewise they haue garden notted bey the letter I. wherin they vse to sowe pompions. Also a place marked with K. wherin the make a fyre att their solemne feasts, and hard without the towne a riuer L. from whence they fetche their water. This people therfore voyde of all couetousnes lyue cherfullye and att their harts ease. Butt they solemnise their feasts in the nigt, and therfore they keepe verye great fyres to auoyde darkenes, ant to testifie their Ioye.

Ther Idol Kivvasa. XXI.

He people of this cuntrie haue an Idol, which they call K I W A S A: yt is carued of woode in lengthe 4. foote whose heade is like the heades of the people of Florida, the face is of a flesh colour, the brest white, the rest is all blacke, the thighes are also spottet with whitte. He hath a chayne abowt his necke of white beades, betweene which are other Rownde beades of copper which they esteeme more then golde or siluer. This Idol is placed in the temple of the towne of Secotam, as the keper of the kings dead corpses. Somtyme they haue two of thes idoles in theyr churches, and somtine 3. but neuer aboue, which they place in a darke corner wher they shew terrible. Thes poore soules haue none other knowledge of god although I thinke them verye Desirous to know the truthe. For when as wee kneeled downe on our knees to make our prayers vnto god, they went abowt to imitate vs, and when they saw we moued our lipps, they also dyd the like. Wherfore that is verye like that they might easelye be brongt to the knowledge of the gospel. God of his mercie grant them this grace.

XXII.

The Tombe of their Werovvans or Cheiff Lordes.

He builde a Scaffolde 9. or 10. foote hihe as is expressed in this figure vnder the tóbs of their Weroans, or cheefe lordes which they couer with matts, and lai the dead corpses of their weroans theruppon in manner followinge. first the bowells are taken forthe. Then layinge downe the skinne, they cutt all the flesh cleane from the bones, which the drye in the sonne, and well dryed the inclose in Matts, and place at their feete. Then their bones (remaininge still fastened together with the ligaments whole and vncorrupted) are couered agayne with leather, and their carcase fashioned as yf their flesh wear not taken away. They lapp eache corps in his owne skinne after thesame in thus handled, and lay yt in his order by the corpses of the other cheef lordes. By the dead bodies they sett their Idol Kiwasa, wher of we spake in the former chapiter: For they are persuaded that thesame doth kepe the dead bodyes of their cheefe lordes that nothinge may hurt them. Moreouer vnder the foresaid scaffolde some on of their preists hath his lodginge, which Mumbleth his prayers nighte and day, and hath charge of the corpses. For his bedd he hath two deates skinnes spredd on the grownde, yf the wether bee cold hee maketh a fyre to warme by withall. Thes poore soules are thus instructed by nature to reuerence their princes euen after their death.

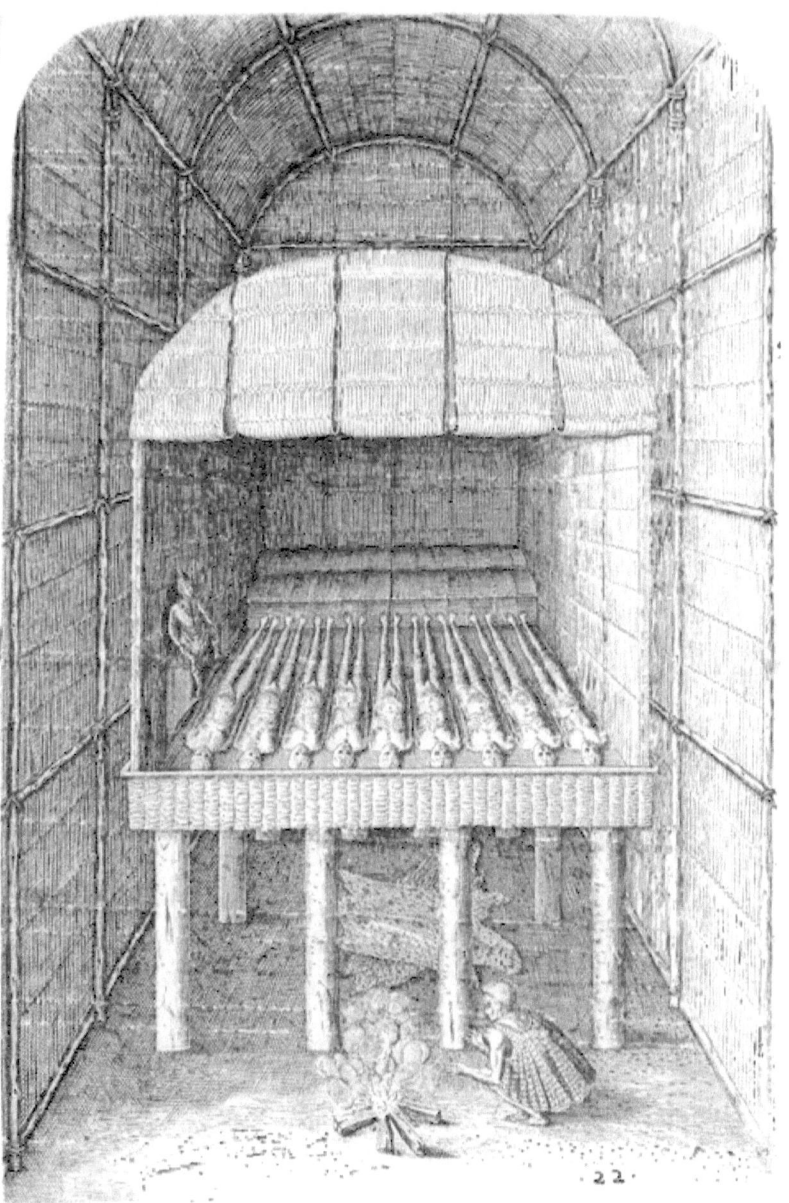

The Marckes of sundrye of the Cheif mene of Virginia.   XXIII.

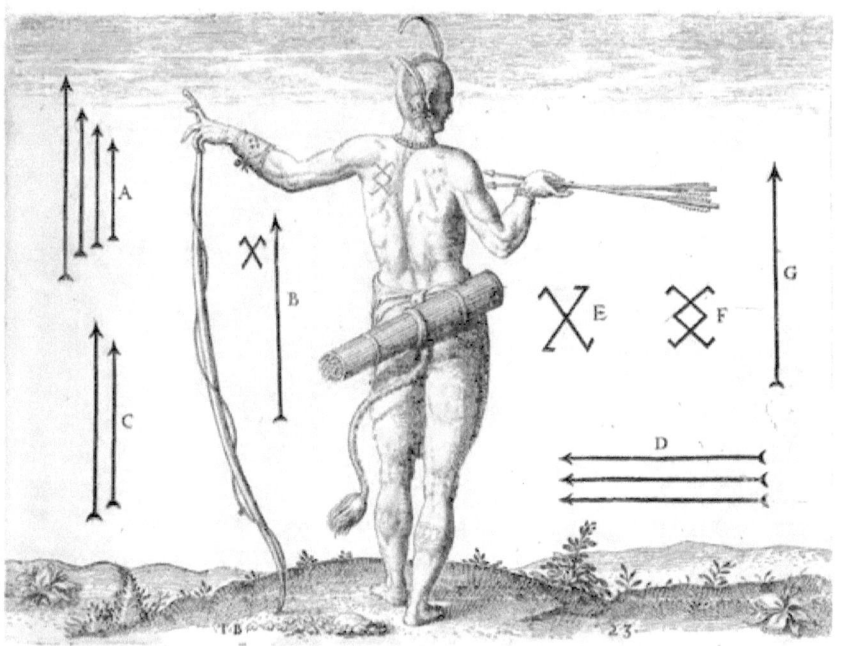

He inhabitâts of all the cuntrie for the most parte haue marks rased on their backs, wherby yt may be knowen what Princes subiects they bee, or of what place they haue their originall. For which cause we haue set downe those marks in this figure, and haue annexed the names of the places, that they might more easelye be discerned. Which industrie hath god indued them withal although they be verye simple, and rude. And to confesse a truthe I cannot remember, that euer I saw a better or quietter people then they.

The marks which I obserued amonge them, are heere put downe in order folowinge.
The marke which is expressed by A. belongeth tho Wingino, the cheefe lorde of Roanoac.
That which hath B. is the marke of Wingino his sisters husbande.
Those which be noted with the letters, of C. and D. belonge vnto diuerse chefe lordes in Secotam.
Those which haue the letters E. F. G. are certaine cheefe men of Pomeiooc, and Aquascogoc.

SOM PICTVRE,
OF THE PICTES
WHICH IN THE OLDE
tyme dyd habite one part of the
great Bretainne.

*THE PAINTER OF WHOM J HAVE
had the first of the Inhabitans of Virginia, giue my allso thees 5. Figures
fallowinge, fownd as by did assured my in a oolld Englush cronicle, the which
I vold well sett to the ende of thees first Figures, for to showe how that
the Inhabitants of the great Bretannie haue bin in ti-
mes past as sauuage as those of
Virginia.*

E

The trvve picture of one Picte I.

IN tymes past the Pictes, habitans of one part of great Bretainne, which is nowe nammed England, wear sauuages, and did paint all their bodye after the maner followinge. the did lett their haire growe as fare as their Shoulders, sauinge those which hange vppon their forehead, the which the did cutt. They shaue all their berde except the mustaches, vppon their breast wear painted the head of som birde, ant about the pappes as yt waere beames of the sune, vppon the bellye sum feere full and monstreus face, spreedinge the beames verye fare vppon the thighes. Vppon the tow knees som faces of lion, and vppon their leggs as yt hath been shelles of fish. Vppon their Shoulders griffones heades, and then they hath serpents abowt their armes: They carted abowt their necks one ayerne ringe, and another abowt the midds of their bodye, abowt the bellye, and the saids hange on a chaine, a cimeterre or turkie soorde, the did carye in one arme a target made of wode, and in the other hande a picke, of which the ayerne was after the manner of a Lick, whith tassels on, and the other ende with a Rounde boule. And when they hath ouercomme some of their ennemis, they did neuer felle to carye awe their heads with them.

The trvve picture of a vvomen Picte II.

THe woemen of the pictes aboue said wear noe worser for the warres then the men. And wear paynted after the manner followinge, hauinge their heads bear, did lett their hairre flyinge. abowt their Showlders wear painted with griffon heades, the lowe parts and thighes with lion faces, or some other beaste as yt commeth best into their fansye, their brest hath a maner of a half moone, with a great stare, and fowre lesser in booth the sides, their pappes painted in maner of beames of the sonne, and amõg all this a great litteninge starre vppon their brests. The saids of som pointes or beames, and the hoolle bellye as a sonne, the armes, thighes, and leggs well painted, of diuerses Figures: The dyd also carye abowt theyr necks an ayern Ringe, as the men did, and suche a girdle with the soorde hainginge, hauinge a Picke or a lance in one hande, and twoe dardz in the other.

The trvve picture of a yonge dowgter of the Pictes I I I.

The yong dougters of the pictes, did also lett their haire flyinge, and wear also painted ouer all the body, so much that noe men could not faynde any different, yf the hath not vse of another fashion of paintinge, for the did paint themselues of sondrye kinds of flours, and of the fairest that they cowld feynde. being fournished for the rest of such kinds of weappon as the woemen wear as you may see by this present picture a thinge trwelly worthie of admiration.

The trvve picture of a man of nation neigbour vnto the Picte   IIII.

THerwas in the said great Bretainne yet another nation nigbour vnto the Pictes, which did apparell them selfues with a kind of cassake other cloath Ierkin, the rest of the bodye wear naked. The did also wear lōge heares, and their moustaches, butt the chin wear also shaued as the other before. The dyd were alardge girdle about them, in which hange a croket soorde, with the target, and did carye the picke or the lance in their hande, which hath at the lowe end a rownde bowlle, as you may see by
this picture.

The trvve picture of a vvomen nigbour to the Pictes   V.

Heir woemen wear apparelled after this manner, butt that their apparell was opne before the breft, and did faftened with a little lefse, as our woemen doe faften their peticott. They lett hange their brefts outt, as for the reft the dyd carye fuche waeppens as the men did, and wear as good as the men for the warre.

A TABLE OF THE PRINCI-
PALL THINGES THAT
are contained in this Historie, after the order of the Alphabet.

A.
Allum	7
Applecrabs	17
Ashe	23
Ascopo.	23

B.
Beares	17
Beech.	23

C.
Cedar	9.23
Chestnuts	17
Ciuet Cattes	9
Conies	19
Coscuhaw	15
Copper	9
Cranes	19
Creuises	21

D.
Deare	19
Deare skinnes	9
Dyes of diuers kindes.	11

E.
Elme.	23

F.
Faulcons	19
Flaxe and Hempe	7
Fiere trees	23
Furres	9

G.
Geese	19
Crappes	17

H.
Habascon	15
Hau they bwild their houses	24
Haukes	19
Hernes	19
Herrings	19
Holly	23
Hurleberies.	17

I.
Iron.	9

K.
Kaishucpenauk	15

The Table.

Kewasowok	26	Popogusso	26
Kewas.	26	Porpoises	16
L.		**R.**	
Leekes	17	Rayes	19
Lions.	19	Rakiock	23
M.		Rafe Lane	32
Macoeqwer	16	Richard Greinuile	32
Mangummenauk	19	Roanoack	8
Maple	23	Rozen	9
Maqwowoc	19	**S.**	
Marlin	19	Sacquenummener	17
Machicomuck	26	Sagatamener and all his kinds	19
Medlars	17	Sapummener	19
Melden	16	Saquenuckot	19
Metaquesunnauk	17	Sassafras	9
Mulberies	17	Sassafras trees	23
Mullets	19	Scalopes	21
Muscles.	21	Seekanauck	21
N.		Sea crabbes	21
Natúre of the Virginiens:	24	Silke of grasse or grasse Silke	7
		Squirels	19
O.		Stockdoues	19
Oade	11	Straberies	17
Of beastes	12	Sturgeons	19
Of foule	19	Suger cannes	11
Of fruites	17	Swannes	19
Of the Vengeance	29	Sweete gummes	11
Okindgier	14	Stones	24
Oldwiues	19	**T.**	
Oyle	9	Tarro	9
Openauk	15	Their manner of fishinge	20
Orepenauk	15	Their manner of makinge boates	20
Oystres.	21	The soyle better	31
P.		The strange oppinion the haue of englishemen	27
Pagatowr	13	The climat of Virginia	31
Parats	19	Their Relligion	25
Partridges	19	Tsinaw	15
Pearle	9	Troutes	19
Periwinckles	21	Tortoyses	21
Pitch	9	Turpentine	9
Plaice	20	Turkie cockes	19
Planta Solis	14.16		Turkie

The Table.

Turkie hennes	19	Wasewowr	11
V.		Weapons of the Virginiens	24
Virginiens willinge to make themselues Christiens.	27	Wichhazle	23
		Wickenzowr	14.16
Virginiens doe estime the things of Europe	27	Wilde peaze.	19
		Willowes	23
Vnknowne sicknes	28	Winauck	9
Vppowoc.	16	Wine	9
W.		Wiroans Wingina	27.28
Walnuts	17	Wiroances	16
Walnut trees	23	Wolues	19
Wapeih	7.8	Worme Silke.	7

F I N I S.

*Faults escaped in the impression. the first nombre signiffie the
page, the second the Linne.*

Pag.11.lin.22 reade, and. pag.14.lin 14.reade sodden. lin.27.reade, about. pag.
16.lin.19.reade, sacrifice. pag.20.lin.18.reade Discouery. pag.23.li.3. reade hatchets.
 In the preface of the figures lin.17.reade lyuely.lin.23.reade late.figure 2.lin.1.
reade wher.lin.7.reade fallinge lin.10. reade neuer. 18. bodye.
 Fig.3.lin 5.reade vppon.fig.7 lin.11 reade and, fig.8.lin.2.reade that. fig.12.lin.
11 reade they.lin.16,reade scrapinge. fig.13.lin. 10. reade also.fig.16.lin.6.drinkinge.
fig.21.lin.12.about.
 The rest if any be the discreete reader may easily amend.

AT FRANCKFORT,
INPRINTED BY IHON WE-
chel, at Theodore de Bry, owne
coast and chardges.

M D XC.

www.ingramcontent.com/pod-product-compliance
Lightning Source LLC
Chambersburg PA
CBHW022135160426
43197CB00009B/1298